£12-50

Staffordshire Blue

W. L. LITTLE

Staffordshire Blue

Underglaze blue transfer-printed earthenware

B. T. Batsford Ltd   London

To D.M.L.

© W. L. Little 1969

First published 1969
Reprinted 1987

Printed and bound in Great Britain by
R. J. Acford Ltd, Chichester, West Sussex
for the publishers B. T. Batsford Ltd
4 Fitzhardinge Street, London W1H 0AH

ISBN 0 7134 5837 2

Contents

Acknowledgment

I AM grateful to my friend Ralph Nye who, having read my original notes and helped to reduce them to intelligible English, encouraged me to continue the study of this branch of English ceramics, which had started only as an interesting exercise, with a view to publication.

I am indebted to the authorities of the Museums named beneath, who have given me much help in study and in obtaining photographs. Special thanks are due to Mr A. R. Mountford, the Director of the City Museum and Art Gallery, Stoke-on-Trent, for allowing me a free run of their very considerable collection of blue transfer-printed earthenwares and for other help.

Thanks are also due to the Bank of England, Mr and Mrs F. Hammond, Mr J. Matthews, O.B.E., Mr and Mrs Thomas Scott and Lieutenant-Colonel T. H. Winterborn, C.B.E., who kindly allowed me to reproduce specimens in their possession.

Mr P. L. Treagus took considerable pains in the photography of specimens in my own collection.

Finally I must thank my publishers B. T. Batsford Ltd. for their patience and helpful advice which has made the publication of this book possible.

W.L.L.

Grateful thanks are due to the following Museums, for permission to reproduce specimens in their possession illustrated in this book:

The City Museums, Stoke-on-Trent, Plates 3, 4, 8, 9, 11, 14, 20, 29, 41, 42, 47, 65, 66, 73, 76, 78, 90, 105 and 109

The Victoria and Albert Museum, Plates 12, 13, 16, 24, 26, 28, 30, 32, 35, 37, 38, 40, 44, 45, 59, 63, 69, 80–82, 92 and 97

The British Museum, Plates 27, 39, 48, 67, 74, 96 and 106

The Bristol City Art Gallery, Plates 93 and 94

The City of Liverpool Museums, Plates 107, 108 and 112

The Sunderland Museum, Plates 114 and 115

Bibliography

Adams, P. W. L., *A History of the Adams Family of North Staffordshire, 1914.*

Bemrose, G., *Nineteenth Century English Pottery and Porcelain, 1952.*

Blacker, J. F., *The ABC of Collecting Old English Pottery.*

Blacker, J. F., *The ABC of Nineteenth Century English Ceramic Art.*

Camehl, A. W., *The Blue China Book, 1948.*

Chaffers, W., *Marks and Monograms on Pottery and Porcelain.*

Cushion, J. P., *Pocket Book of English Ceramic Marks, 1959.*

Earle, A. M., *China Collecting in America, 1892.*

Falkner, F., *The Wood Family of Burslem, 1912.*

Fisher, S. W., *China Collectors Guide.*

Fleming, J. A., *Scottish Pottery, 1923.*

Godden, G. A., *Encyclopaedia of British Pottery and Porcelain Marks, 1964.*

Godden, G. A., *An Illustrated Encyclopaedia of British Pottery and Porcelain, 1966.*

Grant, M. H., *The Makers of Black Basaltes, 1910.*

Haggar, R. G., *English Country Pottery, 1950.*

Hayden, A., *Chats on Old English Earthenware, 1922.*

Hillier, B., *The Turners of Lane End, 1965.*

Honey, W. B., *English Pottery and Porcelain, 1949.*

Hughes, G. B. *English and Scottish Earthenware, 1961.*

Jewitt, L., *The Ceramic Art of Great Britain (2 vols), 1878.*

Kidson, J. R. and F., *Historical Notices of the Leeds Old Pottery, 1892.*

Lancaster, H. B., *Liverpool and her Potters, 1936.*

Mayer, J., *On the Art of Pottery: with a History of its Progress in Liverpool, 1873.*

Moore, N. H., *The Old China Book, 1904.*

Nance, E. M., *The Pottery and Porcelain of Swansea and Nantgarw, 1942.*

Nicholls, R., *Ten Generations of a Potting Family (W. Adams).*

Owen, H., *Two Centuries of Ceramic Art in Bristol, 1873.*

Pountney, W. J., *Old Bristol Potteries, 1920.*

Bibliography

Rhead, G. W., *British Pottery Marks, 1910.*

Rhead, G. W., *The Earthenware Collector, 1920.*

Rhead, G. W. & F. A., *Staffordshire Pots and Potters, 1906.*

Shaw, S., *History of the Staffordshire Potteries, 1829.*

Towner, D. C., *English Cream-coloured Earthenware, 1957.*

Towner, D. C., *The Leeds Pottery, 1963.*

Turner, W., *Transfer Printing on Enamels, Porcelain and Pottery, 1907.*

Turner, W., *William Adams, an Old English Potter, 1923.*

Thorn, J. C., *Handbook of Old Pottery and Porcelain Marks, 1947.*

Wedgwood, J. C., *Staffordshire Pottery and its History.*

Ward, J., *The Borough of Stoke-upon-Trent, 1843.*

Watney, B., *English Blue and White Porcelain of the Eighteenth Century, 1963.*

Westropp, M. S. D., *Irish Pottery and Porcelain (National Museum of Ireland), 1935.*

Williams, S. B., *Antique Blue and White Spode, 1943.*

Preface

THE vast quantities of underglaze blue transfer-printed earthenware produced in the Staffordshire Potteries have led to all blue and white pottery of this description, irrespective of its place of origin, becoming known as 'Staffordshire blue'.

This type of ware has had a great vogue in America, and it still changes hands for large sums. In this country the number of devotees, always substantial, is increasing as the earlier kinds of pottery become scarcer and more expensive.

Little of the early work in the last two decades of the eighteenth century has survived, and the field for the collector lies mainly in the first half of the nineteenth century; many interesting examples of 'Staffordshire blue' being still obtainable at fairly modest prices. Although unsuitable for the cabinet, it looks very well on the shelf, or on the dining room table, and sets of plates and dishes can still be found at a fraction of the cost of a modern dinner service.

At its best it is extremely good technically, and much of it has a quality which is often charming, a charm which has been heightened by the passage of years. Entirely English in origin, it was produced in enormous quantities and was exported all over the world.

This book, largely a work of compilation, attempts to gather together as much as possible of the known information on this type of earthenware. In England, so far as the author knows, no book, with the exception of one on *Antique Blue and White Spode*, has ever been devoted solely to underglaze blue transfer-printed earthenware. It is with the hope that a less esoteric achievement of the English potters may be put on record that this book is written.

The writer would welcome any information about pieces which are illustrated as anonymous and which can be identified by marked specimens in the reader's possession or, indeed, any further observations of interest on marks, or other aspects of the subject.

Introduction

THE last half of the eighteenth century saw the beginning of great social and economic changes in England. The Industrial Revolution, coinciding with the Agricultural Revolution, was in full swing, creating greater wealth and providing more food, clothing and other necessities per head of the population. The population of England and Wales had risen steadily during the eighteenth century from five and a half millions to nine millions. During the last two decades of the century the death rate fell enormously, and by 1830 the population of England, Wales and Scotland had risen from 11 millions to $16\frac{1}{2}$ millions, owing, in large measure, to improved medical services and a greater recognition of the importance of hygiene.

Many families who had been forced to sell their land under the Enclosure of Land Acts, migrated to the towns and flourished in this new and wealthy England and became prosperous in commerce, industry or professional careers. Industrial change began to create varying levels of prosperity and comfort among the working classes. The more skilled working man became the engineer and mechanic, responsible for making and mending the machines. In these early days conditions were less unpleasant, since the full evils attendant upon the Industrial Revolution, which became so manifest by mid-nineteenth century, had not yet fully materialised.

At the same time, there grew up a greater appreciation of art, and admiration of scenery. Towards the end of the eighteenth century arose the great school of artists, chiefly water-colourists, predominantly concerned with depicting landscapes of a more or less topographical character. The literature of the time showed the same trend. Gilbert White, Thomas Bewick, Wordsworth and others prepared the way, and taught their fellow-countrymen to appreciate nature and the charms of rural scenery. The early years of the nineteenth century saw the greatest popularity of the engraved 'colour-print'.

With the Agricultural Revolution had come new techniques in farming. Improved methods of sowing and manuring crops, and breeding and feeding cattle, had brought better and more plentiful food. Cattle and sheep could be kept alive in greater numbers during the winter. Fat stock were reared to a size and weight undreamed of in earlier days. Smallholdings may have disappeared to a large extent, but the tenant farmers prospered.

Scientific invention, together with improved communications provided by better roads and a vast network of waterways, opened up new markets both at home and abroad. The fragile wares of the Staffordshire Potteries could now be easily carried to the ports for shipment overseas. England's supremacy at sea, and clear lead over other nations in machine production, gave her a monopoly of many foreign markets, including America and the Far East. The treaty signed with America in 1783, acknowledging its independence, cleared the way for trade with that country, although it was to be interrupted again by the war of 1812–15. Trade with European markets during the years 1793–1815, when we were at war with France, was spasmodic. In spite of these setbacks the continued increase in population, and improving conditions, created a larger market for all manufacturers.

This was a period of evolution, with industry moving towards mass production. It could now supply necessities for all classes, instead of concentrating on luxuries for the well-to-do. As the nineteenth century advanced, so were the amenities of life improved. Families were larger, domestic servants were plentiful and cheap; pewter went out of general use, and dinner services as we know them came to stay. Tea was beginning to replace milk and beer as the main drink of the working classes, and hot cooked meals began to be enjoyed by a larger section of the community. The opportunity to satisfy the increasing demand for domestic wares, first exploited by Josiah Wedgwood with his cream-coloured 'Queen's Ware', was later eagerly followed by the Staffordshire potters, with their newer and cheaper white earthenware bodies decorated with underglaze blue printing. The very well-to-do still favoured their porcelain services, but the blue and white earthenware, used at first by merchants and professional classes, soon came within reach of ordinary purses. As prices became lower, it was an exciting novelty for the masses to be able to eat from a more decorative table ware. As demand expanded, so the potters became more ambitious and competitive. They strove for the perfect mechanical finish, and sought to reproduce every conceivable variation of engraved pattern on their services. For a time 'blue-printed' practically superseded every other type of earthenware, and was distributed throughout the world.

But towards the middle of the nineteenth century over-production inevitably led to a decay in style. Workmanship became shoddy, and the quality of the prints deteriorated. Although some good work persisted, other developments intervened, and the experiments in underglaze printing in different colours, which had been carried on for some time, now resulted in a product which rapidly overtook blue printing in popularity.

The Invention and Development
of Transfer-printing

THE centuries-old process by which designs were engraved on copper, and reproduced in quantity on paper, was first adapted as a means of decorating pottery shortly after the middle of the eighteenth century. It was one of the few entirely British contributions to the potter's art, and one that became of immense importance to the ceramic industry. This was an age when industry generally was looking for methods of producing cheaper wares, in larger quantities, by mechanical processes. Until this time, the only means known to the potter of applying coloured decoration was by hand painting: an alternative to this comparatively laborious and expensive method, such as transfer-printing, would be readily accepted.

Independent experiments had presumably been carried out for some years before its successful application. Most authorities now agree, on the evidence available, that the credit for the first successful use of the process must be awarded to John Brooks, an Irish engraver. His first application for a patent for printing on enamels and china was dated 10 September 1751, when he was living in Birmingham. It appears likely, therefore, that his first printing on enamels and chinaware was practised at Birmingham. In 1753 he was registered as a partner in the firm of Janssen, Delamain & Brooks, at the enamel factory at York House, Battersea, London. Exactly how long the active life of this manufactory lasted is not certain, but the stock and the equipment were sold up by auction in June 1756. During its short life it is known that Brooks was employed in producing transfer-prints on the enamel surfaces of small boxes and other articles.

Robert Hancock was another engraver who played an important part in the history of transfer-printing on china. He also began work in Birmingham, and served his apprenticeship to George Anderton, an engraver of that town. Controversy has always raged among the experts as to whether he actually worked at Battersea, although much of his work is said to have been identified on Battersea enamels. The latest evidence seems to lead to the conclusion that all his work was done in the Midlands.*

* The evidence is summed up in papers by Bernard Watney and R. J. Charleston, *E.C.C. Trans.* vol. 6, part 2

What appears to be more certain is that he went to Worcester in late 1756, or early 1757: here he produced his best work, and transfer-printing began to form an important part of the output of the Worcester porcelain factory.

Almost simultaneously the process had been developed by John Sadler, a printer and engraver, and his partner Guy Green, both of Liverpool. Their experiments had been brought to such a successful conclusion that, on 27 July 1756, they were able to print within the space of six hours 'upwards of twelve hundred earthenware tiles of different patterns at Liverpoole aforesaid, and which, as these deponents have heard and believe, were more in number, and better, and neater than one hundred skilful pot painters could have painted in the like space of time, in the common and usual way of painting with a pencil; and these deponents say that they have been upwards of seven years in finding out the method of printing tiles, and in making tryals and experiments for that purpose, which they have now, through great pains and expense brought to perfection.'*

For many years Sadler & Green carried on their printing works, decorating wares for the Liverpool potters. The Staffordshire potters, especially Josiah Wedgwood, sent large quantities of their cream-coloured earthenware to Liverpool to be decorated in this way.

It is conceivable that Sadler was inspired by the same source as Battersea. Henry Delamain, one of the Battersea proprietors, was almost certainly the same Henry Delamain, a maker of delftware in Dublin, who, on 1 November 1753, had presented a petition to the Irish House of Commons, in which he stated that he had 'purchased the art of printing earthenware with as much beauty, strong impression and dispatch as can be done on paper'.† Liverpool, as a port and one of the centres of delftware manufacture, had regular trade relations with Ireland; both Dublin and Liverpool used clay from Carrickfergus for their pottery,‡ and Delamain is known to have been in Liverpool in December 1753.§

In these early days, transfer-prints were always applied to the fired glaze, i.e. overglaze transfer-printed. They were printed in enamel colours, mainly black, sometimes in brick red, and somewhat later in various shades of brown and purple. It was not possible to apply them to the biscuit ware before glazing, i.e. underglaze transfer-printing, as the colours would not survive the high temperature of the glost oven without losing their original value. Trials were made with other colours, but in these early days the only colour which could be applied with complete success under the glaze was blue, a pigment prepared from cobalt oxide. This colouring matter, as was already known from its use in underglaze blue painting, could withstand, and indeed required, the higher fluxing temperature of the glost oven. The overglaze print gave greater clarity of detail but, lacking the protection of the glaze, was less durable, and

* Joseph Mayer, *On the Art of Pottery: with a History of its Progress in Liverpool*, 1873, pp. 56–7
† M. S. D. Westropp, *National Museum of Ireland. Irish Pottery and Porcelain*, Dublin, 1935, p. 12
‡ Westropp, *op. cit.*, p. 11
§ Westropp, *op. cit.*, p. 15

lacked the rich soft effect given by the glaze to the blue beneath. Underglaze printing had the added advantage of requiring one less firing process.

Underglaze blue printing on porcelain had been introduced at Worcester by 1760. Bow used the same technique, but only sparingly, at about the same time; other porcelain factories followed suit. Richard Holdship, one of the partners of the Worcester factory, and manager of their printing department, went to Derby in 1764: he signed an agreement with Messrs Duesbury & Heath of that factory in which he undertook to reveal not only formulae for manufacturing porcelain bodies but also the art of overglaze and underglaze transfer-printing, but very little use of his services was made (pl. 1). Soon after 1770, underglaze blue printing was used at Lowestoft. It was tried at Bristol on hard paste porcelain, but was abandoned owing to technical difficulties. The Worcester factory made great use of the process; later the Caughley works, under Thomas Turner, used it to an even greater extent.

Thomas Turner, an engraver and practical potter, was born in 1749. He worked for some time at the Worcester Porcelain factory with Robert Hancock, but left there in 1772 to become Ambrose Gallimore's partner in a small pottery at Caughley, near Broseley, in Shropshire. This pottery had existed since about 1750 and had always made earthenwares. It was Turner's object to enlarge it, and produce substantial quantities of blue and white porcelain. This he had successfully achieved by 1775, when a local newspaper stated that the works had been completed, and large orders for porcelain had been received and fulfilled.* By then he appears to have taken over complete control of the factory, and gathered together a competent school of assistant and apprentice engravers and printers. Robert Hancock, who had given up his share in the Worcester works, also joined him about this time.

Earthenware still continued to be made at Caughley, and it was here that underglaze blue printing was first used on this type of ware. Traditionally, the 'Willow' pattern, designed in 1780 by Thomas Minton, an apprentice engraver working at Caughley, is regarded as the first pattern to be transfer-printed on earthenware. This was one of the many Anglo-oriental designs based on variations of Chinese motifs to appear on earthenware, similar to those which had previously been used on early English porcelains. Taken up by the Staffordshire potteries, this underglaze transfer-printing, originated in Shropshire, was to become famous throughout the world as 'Staffordshire blue'.

The leading Staffordshire potters quickly realised the commercial possibilities of this new technique for decorating earthenware, and appear to have lost no time in trying to attract skilled craftsmen from Caughley and elsewhere. Ralph Baddeley of Shelton had been active since about 1777 with experiments in overglaze and bat-printing, but although helped by William Smith, an engraver from Liverpool, and later by Thomas Davis, a printer from Worcester, had not reached a successful conclusion with underglaze blue until about 1782. William Adams of Cobridge had been making

* Chaffers, *Marks and Monograms*, 14th Edn., 1932, p. 766

similar trials, aided by William Davis of Worcester and Caughley, and was more successful. He may well have been the first to introduce blue printing into Staffordshire. In 1783, Josiah Spode employed Thomas Lucas, an engraver, and James Richards, a printer, both from Caughley: he is said to have been completely successful by 1784, and was probably the largest producer at that time. John Yates of Shelton, another potter early in the printing field, secured the services of John Ainsworth, also of Caughley, in 1783, but little more is heard of him in this connection. William Adams of Greengates, probably with the help of his Cobridge cousin, achieved success by 1787, and three years later was one of the leading producers. The smaller potteries soon followed the example of the leading potters, and the use of this new and cheaper method of decoration quickly spread, and in time was to become almost universal.

The cream-coloured wares decorated with painting or overglaze enamel printing, which had enjoyed such a long run, began to lose ground. Records of the time show that, although very few potters were listed as blue printers in the 1780s, their number had greatly increased by the end of the century. Had sufficient qualified engravers and printers been available, the spread of blue printing would doubtless have been even quicker. Like all new mechanical processes it had encountered opposition—in this case, as would be expected, from the painters who thought it would endanger their own particular skills. The first Josiah Wedgwood, who died in 1795, had been responsible for introducing more innovations in the ceramic industry than any other single man. He had met a certain amount of resistance when he started to decorate his Queen's Ware with overglaze printing. Shaw records that when underglaze blue printing was introduced, Wedgwood was approached by his enamel painters with an urgent request to prevent its use. He is said to have replied: 'I have not made, neither will I make, any Blue Printed Earthenware.'* No doubt he thought that blue printing did not measure up to the high standard of the other wares for which, by then, he was famous; and, in fact, no blue-printed pottery was made at Etruria until the time of the second Josiah Wedgwood.

By 1810, blue-printed earthenware was being produced in large quantities, and was to bring great prosperity to the Potteries. Soon after 1815, with the end of the Napoleonic War and the signing of the peace treaty with America, a growing export trade was resumed with Europe and the United States. A directory of earthenware potters, compiled in 1818 by W. Parson and T. Bradshaw and printed by Leigh of Manchester, lists 144 master potters in the Staffordshire Potteries.† It is unlikely that many of them, engaged in making table services and similar wares, could afford not to make blue-printed. This is confirmed by Shaw's experience when, writing his *History of the Staffordshire Potteries*, published in 1829, the material for which was gathered over several years, he said: 'For the novelty and elegance of the Pottery secured the demand, which has continued to increase; and in this day, 1829, few

---

* Simeon Shaw, *History of the Staffordshire Potteries*, 1829, p. 193
† Josiah Wedgwood, *Staffordshire Pottery and its History*, pp. 152–6

manufacturers do not practise the art; and many have several presses constantly employed in Blue Printing.'*

From about 1820 to 1840 was the period of peak production, when blue-printed was being exported all over the world. A complete list of all firms engaged in making these printed wares at any time from its inception up to the middle of the nineteenth century, if it were possible to compile it, would probably number over 500. Other pottery centres such as Hull, Leeds, Liverpool and Swinton in the North, and Bristol and Swansea in the West, also produced much excellent blue-printed ware. In addition, other potters in Newcastle, Sunderland and Scotland used this method of decoration.

As already stated, by 1840 blue printing had a formidable rival in colour printing, and its popularity began to wane. Attempts to produce underglaze printing in colours other than blue had been made since the end of the eighteenth century. Early success was achieved with brown and black. The small pottery of David Dunderdale at Castleford, and others, were producing an excellent underglaze brown between 1810 and 1820. From about 1825 other colours were being used, and by 1835 probably more green- and pink- than blue-printed wares were being exported to America. Perhaps even before this it was beginning to lose caste at home. Speaking of colour printing, Shaw, in his usual rather sycophantic style, records at the end of his book that 'this pottery has a rich and delicate appearance, and owing to the Blue printed having become so common, the other is now obtaining a decided preference in most genteel circles'.†

In addition, many more potters were making porcelain which was becoming cheaper, and consequently coming into more general use. By 1850, Staffordshire blue had had its day. Colour printing finally superseded it, although never becoming so popular in this country as the blue had been. This preference will be shared by most collectors. Very many specimens of underglaze blue made after this time are to be seen, but they are all, with few exceptions, of poor quality and badly printed. In modern times a few firms have revived some of the old patterns with excellent results.

* Shaw, *op. cit.*, p. 215
† Shaw, *op. cit.*, p. 235

The Technical Development
of Staffordshire Blue

THE complete success eventually attained by the potters in producing technically perfect underglaze transfer-prints depended very largely on the engravers. The traditional method for producing prints on paper had to be modified when the copper plate was to be used for the additional process of transferring a clear impression of the pattern from the paper to a pottery surface. One great advantage was that the design could be engraved on the metal plate exactly as it was to appear on the finished article. The double process of transferring the print from the plate to the paper, and then from the paper to the pottery, resulted in the print appearing in the positive.

Except in subject, the early underglaze prints on porcelain differed very little in engraving technique from the earlier enamel overglaze prints. Shading, and other effects, were produced by a series of close parallel lines and cross-hatching. The blue colour had more body than the overglaze enamels, but was affected first by sinking into the porous biscuit body, and again by being softened by the glaze melting over it. This caused a somewhat blurred and smudged effect in which the detail of the print was partly lost. The first underglaze prints on earthenware were carried out on much the same lines, and large areas were left plain white. The engraved lines had to be thickly cut in order that sufficient colour could be transferred to the paper for re-transfer to the pottery. Later, when the quality of the paper had been improved, a better result was obtained by cutting thinner lines, more deeply. Further variety was obtained by cutting the lines on the copper plate to different depths. The greatest improvement came early in the nineteenth century when pure line engraving was combined with stipple engraving. By adding the use of the burr to that of the graver, not only were fine-tone gradations in colour obtained, but completely new effects with shading covering nearly all the surface of the design, and giving the rich soft effect of a water colour. At about the same time a new method of transferring continuous strip borders of repeat patterns came into use.

The process of transferring the print from the copper plate to the ware remained basically the same over the whole period, although many technical improvements were introduced with experience. The engraved plate was warmed over a stove, and the colour, mixed into a stiff paste with oil, was worked well into the incised pattern. All the excess colour was scraped off with a palette knife, and the surface of the plate further cleaned with a pad or boss. A sheet of paper, softened with soap and water, was laid over the design on the copper plate and subjected to the action of a press. By this means the paper was forced into close contact with the colour and received a clear impression of the engraving. The copper plate was replaced on the stove and warmed sufficiently for the paper to be peeled off without damage to the print. Any superfluous paper was cut away, and the transfer applied to the biscuit ware in the required position and rubbed evenly by hand with a soaped flannel, ensuring that any joins in the paper were accurately made; the friction caused the oil-bound colour to adhere to the surface. The ware was then immersed in water, and the paper carefully removed, so that the impression was not injured. Previous to glazing, the piece was placed in a low-temperature kiln and heated sufficiently to dry out the oil, and 'harden on' the colour. The biscuit ware was now ready to be dipped into the glaze. This was a mixture of various materials, diluted with water to the consistency of cream. The porous biscuit would absorb sufficient water to hold the glaze, and on removal from the glaze, all traces of the transfer-printed pattern would have disappeared. The firing in the glost oven reduced the glaze to a glass-like covering, disclosing again the pattern underneath.

The greatest advance in the quality of the prints was due to a new machine for making tissue-paper, introduced into this country by the Fourdrinier family, who had been engaged for many years in improving the process of papermaking. Henry Fourdrinier (1766–1854), after whom the machine is now always named, owned a mill at Dartford in Kent, and erected the first machine at Frogmore in Berkshire in 1803. This machine produced a thin, strong tissue-paper, to replace the coarser paper then in use for transfer-printing. In 1827, the Fourdriniers moved to the Ivy House Paper Mill, Hanley, Staffordshire, in order to supply more easily the enormous demand which had grown up in the Potteries for transfer papers. The patent for this invention was apparently infringed by other paper makers, and in 1839 the House of Commons took the unusual step of granting the Fourdrinier firm £7,000 as compensation. The Committee in their report stated that this 'extraordinary invention has enabled the Earthenware Manufacturers to increase the beauty and accuracy of their patterns by the aid of a superior kind of tissue-paper; has enabled the lithographic and other engravers, paper stainers, and publishers greatly to improve their arts.'* There is little doubt that, without this improved transfer paper, the Staffordshire blue trade could never have reached the enormous proportions which it did. J. & R. Clews of Cobridge, who commenced potting in 1818 and specialised in this type of work, recorded in 1820: 'Had not this improvement taken place, the new style of engraving would have been useless, as the paper previously used was too coarse

* John Ward, *The Borough of Stoke-upon-Trent*, London, 1843, p. 376

to draw from the engraved plate anything like a clear or perfect impression. An astonishing improvement took place in printing both on china and earthenware, more particularly the latter.'

The development of a suitable type of earthenware body was essential to display the true brilliance of the underglaze cobalt blue. A cream-coloured earthenware had been in general use for many years, especially since Josiah Wedgwood had perfected his Queen's Ware about 1765. It had been the constant aim of the earthenware potters to produce a white ware. This had been partially achieved in the past with tin-enamel glazed delftware and salt-glazed wares, but these had many disadvantages in use. In 1775 the Staffordshire potters, headed by Josiah Wedgwood, opposed the application of Richard Champion of Bristol for an extension of the term of patent right for the sole use of china clay and china stone. This patent had originally been granted to William Cookworthy in 1768 for the manufacture of his hard paste porcelain at Plymouth, and had been taken over by Champion in 1774. Although Champion was granted his extension, he was only given the sole and exclusive use of these Cornish materials for the manufacture of transparent wares. This meant that any other potter had the free use of them for the manufacture of opaque pottery. In 1779 Wedgwood introduced a fine white earthenware, which he called 'pearl ware'. It contained a greater proportion of calcined ground flint and white Cornish china clay than the creamware, and a minute quantity of cobalt blue in the glaze and body, to counteract any discolouration caused by particles of iron in the clay. Pearl ware was the precursor of all the white earthenwares of later times. It was a body of this type which Turner at Caughley, and the Staffordshire potters, used for their first attempts at underglaze printing on earthenware. Champion's patent had finally expired in 1796, when the Cornish materials became available to potters for any purpose. In addition, a high tariff had been levied upon imported porcelain in 1794. These events gave new momentum to further experiments, but the fullest development did not take place until the nineteenth century. After many experiments, Josiah Spode II introduced his stone china about 1805. This was a much stronger, more durable body than pearl ware, with a good lustrous glaze. C. J. Mason invented his 'Ironstone China', for which a patent was granted in 1813. It was a hard, immensely strong, heavy and inexpensive ware. During the next decade or two, a number of new bodies were evolved. They were mostly good, serviceable, resonant wares, varying in texture and weight, covered with hard, brilliant glazes, less apt to show scratches. Many of them masqueraded as porcelain under such names as semi, and opaque china, or porcelain.

The numbers of those engaged in ancillary trades increased in proportion with the demand for Staffordshire blue. These included dealers in earthenware, packers, clay agents and colour makers, and cobalt refiners. Cobalt has always been essential as the agent for blue decoration, whether painted or printed, and cobalt blue is the oldest known pigment used for ceramic decoration. The two manufactured products of cobalt are zaffre and smalt; zaffre is an impure oxide of cobalt, the residuum when certain volatile matters have been expelled by calcination: smalt is a more purified form of the same material, fused to form a dark blue glass. The potters used either zaffre or smalt, finely pulverised to a powder, for underglaze blue printing. Smalt, being more carefully prepared, was more costly and gave the better colour, a richer deeper blue, although, from the point of view of the collector, uncertain variations in colour can often be more attractive than the more controlled, sometimes almost harsh colour of the more refined and purer cobalt. In the main, the English potters were dependent on good quality smalt and zaffre imported from Saxony and Sweden. Deposits of cobalt were found from time to time in Cornwall. William Cookworthy of Plymouth, a trained chemist, is said to have been the first to manufacture cobalt blue direct from the ore in this country.* Shaw relates how Cookworthy instructed Roger Kinnaston on the process of preparing zaffre and smalt and how, with his help, the latter set up a cobalt smelting works at Cobridge about 1772.† Later, in the early nineteenth century, Burslem became an important centre for the refining of cobalt ore and zaffre.‡ In 1799 Louis Jacques Thénard (1777–1857), a French chemist, prepared an artificial ultramarine, a cheap colouring matter capable of standing the heat of the kiln. This was known as 'Thénard's blue' and is said to have been imported into England by 1802; but to what extent it was used is difficult to say.

The first half of the nineteenth century was a period rich in inventions for the improvement of the ceramic industry generally. Three times as many patents were registered during this time than in the previous 200 years. These included many improvements in bodies and glazes, potters' ovens and kilns, and several in connection with printing. In 1831 a patent was granted to John Potts, Richard Oliver and William Wainwright Potts, calico printers of New Mills Works, near Derby, for a rotary press for printing transfer papers from revolving steel cylinders. In 1833, W. W. Potts became a partner in the firm of Machin & Potts at the Waterloo Pottery, Burslem, where the new machine was extensively employed for printing on pottery.

Special processes were introduced to extract impurities from the clays, in order that they should be as white as possible. Many improvements were made in the kilns. It was important that temperatures should be regulated exactly, as this was a decisive factor in controlling the colour of the underglaze blue during the firing in the glost oven.

An innovation was devised, apparently at some time in the 1820s, known as 'flowing' or 'flown blue', and was used in many factories. Cups containing a volatilising mixture, such as lime, or chloride of ammonia, were placed in the saggers during the glaze firing, causing the colour to run slightly. It was thought to produce a softer effect, and reduce the mechanical look of the print. It had the desired effect with some of the lighter blue patterns, but many of the pieces printed in a very deep blue have run to such an extent that the design has been almost completely obscured (pl. 46).

* L. C. Jewitt, *A Life of Josiah Wedgwood*, 1865, p. 232
† Shaw, *op. cit.*, p. 211
‡ Ward, *op. cit.*, p. 266

Dinner and dessert services, tea-sets and toilet wares were turned out in enormous quantities to satisfy demand at home and abroad. The number of covers increased as families grew larger. Serving dishes of all sizes were made for meat, game and fish, the latter including a strainer. Soup, vegetable and gravy tureens, and sauce-boats came in all shapes, with knobs and handles of every design. Services, which in the early days had been printed with different sizes of the same pattern, later had as many as 10–15 different views printed on the various pieces. Each flat piece carried one picture: hollow ware often had several different pictures on inner and outer surfaces. Owing to the different shapes and sizes, many copper plates of each pattern had to be engraved for each service. It was only the facility with which the extensive range of these elaborate patterns could be applied, by means of transfer-printing, that made this vast output an economic possibility.

The Engravings and their Sources

THE designs used by Thomas Turner of Caughley for engraving on his early underglaze blue-printed earthenware were, naturally enough, the same type of *chinoiseries* (pl. 2) previously used by him, and other factories, on porcelain. The practice of the eighteenth-century English potters of imitating imported Chinese wares was to die hard. As already mentioned, the Willow pattern is traditionally regarded as the first design to be produced in underglaze blue on earthenware. This design, said to have been engraved by Thomas Minton whilst serving his apprenticeship at Caughley, enjoyed enormous popularity, and was copied, with variations, by almost every other potter. The remarkable appeal made by the Willow pattern has seemingly lasted and ensured its continuity, on the commoner types of ware, right up to the present day. Another pattern said to have been engraved by Minton at Caughley in 1782 was the 'Broseley dragon'. This was named after the village near which the factory was situated. The Staffordshire potters soon followed suit with versions of these and other patterns, based on Chinese motifs. The engravers often failed to grasp the meaning of oriental symbolism and conventions, but usually arrived at a happy solution by supplying details from their own imagination.

Thomas Minton, shortly after completing his apprenticeship at Caughley, moved to London and worked as an engraver for Josiah Spode at his warehouse in Portugal Street. Evidently anticipating the great demand for this new type of decoration, he moved, about 1788, to the centre of the industry, and set up as a master engraver at Stoke-on-Trent. He was probably the first to specialise in the engraving of copper plates for the Staffordshire blue printing trade. He produced many designs, including different versions of the Willow and Broseley patterns for Spode, and other potters. Another of his patterns used by Spode was the 'Buffalo': this was also used by J. Heath of Hanley (pl. 31). Minton remained in the engraving and printing trade until he established his own pottery at Stoke in 1793, and founded the firm which still flourishes today.

Many of the early prints were produced at the factory of the master potter concerned, by engravers enticed from Caughley, Worcester or Liverpool. Engraving shops for engraving and printing designs for overglaze prints had existed in the Potteries for some time. In a list quoted by Chaffers of 'Trades in connection with potters in 1802', many are still listed as black printers; others are shown as engravers, and these were almost certainly largely engaged in producing designs for the well-established and rapidly growing 'blue-printed' trade.

Nearly all engravings, wherever they were produced, are anonymous. Occasionally a name appears incorporated in the transfer design: that of John Martin of Shelton is sometimes seen on a design, and is almost certainly the name of the engraver and not of the potter. The adjoining towns of Hanley and Shelton, united into one town by act of Parliament in 1812, were an important centre for this trade. Bentley, Wear & Bourne (subsequently Bentley & Wear) of Vine Street, Shelton, operating from 1815 onwards, were a firm of engravers and printers whose name sometimes occurs as part of the design (pl. 39). Shaw, writing in 1829, gave an interesting note about this firm: 'In Vine Street, Shelton, Messrs Bentley & Wear, eminent engravers, have a fine Gallery of Paintings, including some of considerable value, the productions of early Artists; but useful to the district as a Depot of the work of resident artists.'[*] Ward, writing 14 years later, noted that: 'The business of engraving for the use of the manufacturers is extensively practised in Hanley and Shelton, and gives employment to a considerable number of artists, of whom some have risen to eminence in the higher department of the art.'[†] Another Shelton artist of a later date, whose signature is occasionally found on printed patterns, is James Cutts, not to be confused with John Cutts, the last proprietor of the Pinxton China factory, who left there in 1813 to set up his own decorating establishment in Hanley. John Aynsley of Lane End, one of the earlier engravers, is well known for his signature on black overglaze prints. It seems unlikely that he did not produce some copper plates for blue printing, but none appear to have been signed. William Brooke(s) of Tunstall, a well-known engraver, did some early work for the Adams factory at Greengates. He is credited by Shaw with making the original suggestion, about 1802, for ornamenting the borders of blue-printed wares by using continuous strips of repeat patterns similar to those then in fashion for wallpaper hangings of rooms—a practice which was soon adopted generally by all potters.

Probably nearly all of the anonymous engravings were by artists now long forgotten, and perhaps not of much account even in their own day. However, the sources from which the designs were copied are much more widely known. The Europeanised oriental scenes appear to have satisfied the public taste until early in the nineteenth century. Little originality was displayed until after 1805. Perhaps the Battle of Trafalgar, and the removal of the shadow of invasion, gave the required impetus. After all national crises people demand change and novelty. A growing middle class in the towns, a result of the Industrial Revolution, provided the potters with the neces-

[*] Shaw, *op. cit.*, p. 46
[†] Ward, *op. cit.*, p. 381

sary market. Table wares with decorative pictures on them, in place of the too-familiar *chinoiseries*, were a welcome change. The firm of Spode was perhaps the first to break away from the oriental convention. Jewitt lists 37 patterns which this factory introduced over a period of 20 years, starting in 1806.* This list, whether entirely accurate or not, and difficult in some cases to identify, does provide some sort of clue as to the approximate dates at which various types of pattern made their appearance. The most original, and the first scenic pictures on pottery, were his Italianate series including such patterns as Lucano (pl. 61), and Tower, Tiber and Castle (pl. 60). These designs were all derived from engravings published in 1797–8 in J. Merigots' *Views and Rivers in Rome and its Vicinity.* The fashionable Grand Tour of the Continent in the eighteenth century often included an artist, whose paintings were engraved and produced in book form. Other books with *Views in Asia Minor, mainly in Caramania, Views in Egypt, Palestine and the Ottoman Empire* and *Views in Egypt,* all published at the end of the eighteenth, or early in the nineteenth century, provided material for the engravers, as sources for their prints for the potters, each producing a different result. These contemporary travel books set the fashion for scenes with romantic ruins, and were produced by many potters. The 'Blue Italian' pattern, one of the early Spode designs, which their successors W. T. Copeland & Sons Ltd. have chosen to perpetuate, was originally derived from a similar source. Classical landscapes after the school of Claude appear with the marks of Benjamin Adams (pl. 4), J. & R. Riley (pl. 52) and others. Another entirely original idea by Spode was the 'Indian Sporting' series (pl. 62), probably introduced soon after 1810. Not only was the subject a completely new one, but many different pictures were engraved on the same service, as opposed to the usual single pattern. These were taken from drawings by the landscape and animal painter Samuel Howitt (1765–1822) illustrating *Oriental Field Sports, Wild Sports of the East* by Captain Thomas Williamson, published in various forms between 1805 and 1807. Of about the same period were Spode's simple patterns, 'Nankin' and 'Lange Lizsen', literal copies of Chinese K'ang Hsi blue and white porcelain. These were followed by pastoral scenes such as 'The Milkmaid', 'The Woodman', 'Girl at the Well' and others. A detailed study of the engravings produced by this firm, by S. B. Williams, was published in 1943 in *Antique Blue and White Spode.* This appears to be the only monograph ever published in this country devoted solely to blue transfer-printed wares.

Once this new ground had been broken, and with an increasing number of potters engaging in this branch of the trade, novelty of design became the primary consideration. Between 1810 and 1840, patterns of an extraordinarily diverse and varied nature made their appearance. Very few subjects escaped the potters' attention, and almost any print was considered suitable as a medium for decoration. These were copied and adapted, sometimes with incongruous results, but usually with originality and charm. Illustrations were copied from any source without acknowledgment.

* Jewitt, *op. cit.,* vol. 2, pp. 183–4

Copyright laws were then extremely lax; the Registration of Designs Act did not come into force until 1842.

Romantic pastoral landscapes had a tremendous vogue (pl. 64), as also did senti-mental domestic genre subjects. Each potter produced his own patterns, often un-named, others with titles printed on the back such as 'Game keeper', 'Hop Pickers' (pl. 91), 'Pastoral scene' (pl. 46), etc. Sporting prints of the chase (pl. 118), others show-ing sportsmen with gun (pl. 109), rod (pl. 100) or bow (pl. 68) were copied, and some, very rare alas, of celebrated cricket matches. Some potters specialised in floral designs and botanical sprays, others in shipping or livestock. One potter produced a series of famous fatstock. The 'Durham Ox' (pl. 88) was copied from an engraving by J. Whessell after a painting by T. Boultbee, published in 1802. Another series was called 'Domestic Cattle' (pl. 90).

At the beginning of the nineteenth century, the traditional taste of connoisseurs for classical compositions began to change to a preference for portraits of country mansions and views of well-known places. This was the great age of the English water-colourists. They toured the British Isles making careful topographical landscape drawings: abbeys, castles, cathedrals, colleges and other places of interest were painted by the hundred. Many of these were engraved, and appeared in illustrated books. The potters made full use of them and, about 1815, began to pass this change of taste on to the masses in the shape of decorated earthenware. Several hundreds of these named scenic views by various potters have been recorded. Some of them were taken from engravings by William Wallis (fl. 1815), after drawings by Thomas H. Shepherd; others from engravings by J. Shury (fl. 1812), after H. West. A print of the Bank of England produced by Enoch Wood & Sons was taken from an engraving by William Tombleson after a drawing by Shepherd published in 1827. Another print of the Bank was produced by William Adams. A lengthy search for examples of these prints, carried out by correspondence and advertising in 1938 both in England and America, failed to locate a single specimen by Adams, and only two by Wood, both in America: one of these is now in the Bank of England collection (pl. 77). An interesting series of colleges and important buildings in Oxford and Cambridge was produced by J. & W. Ridgway (pl. 50). Some of the views of Oxford were painted by Edward Dayes (1763–1804) and were first engraved for the *Oxford Almanac* in 1800: some of these were republished in 1820 engraved by J. Skelton.

The early English views were closely followed by even more numerous views of American buildings and scenery. The old-established firms of William Adams of Stoke and Enoch Wood were almost certainly the first in the field with the English views. Enoch Wood probably took the lead with American views. Both potters used a dark blue and set the fashion for this new deep rich colour. They were soon followed by well-known, but more recently established firms, such as R. Stevenson, J. & W. Ridgway, J. & R. Riley, A. Stevenson and J. & R. Clews. From the evidence supplied by the dates of these firms, it would seem certain that the English views began to ap-

pear before the American ones. Factories established after 1820 seem for the most part
to have concentrated on American views only, first in blue and later in other underglaze colours. Curiously enough, some of the large firms such as Spode and Minton,
which had taken such a leading part in the development of underglaze printing did
not produce any named English or American views. This was presumably because they
had by this time begun to specialise in their more sophisticated wares, in both earthenware and porcelain. This American export trade was to assume tremendous importance during the next 15–20 years.

Soon after 1783, when the independence of our American colonies had been
acknowledged by the Treaty of Versailles, the Liverpool potters had started a brisk
export trade with them. With a fine disregard for any feelings of patriotic pride, they
conceived the idea of embellishing their wares with black enamel overglaze prints of
American heroes, and scenes celebrating American triumphs. As has been said, this
trade was interrupted by the unnecessary war with America from 1812–15. Before
this war, quite large quantities of the early patterns on the new blue underglaze
printed wares must have been shipped to America along with creamwares and porcelain. Soon after the peace treaty the Staffordshire potters decided that a most profitable
trade might be resumed with the United States in the same wares that had become so
popular in England, adapting them to indulge the civic pride of a new and conquering
nation, by portraying scenes showing their military and naval triumphs, as well as
using engravings of American buildings and scenery. Designs were reproduced from
volumes of contemporary prints or from sketches made on the spot by travelling
artists or tourists. A series from a volume of *Beauties of America* was produced by
J. & W. Ridgway. W. G. Wall, an Irish artist, went to the United States in 1818 and
supplied many drawings to Andrew Stevenson of Cobridge. His name appears on the
back of at least 12 designs as part of a blue-printed mark in addition to the impressed
mark A. STEVENSON. In 1823 a set of Wall's drawings was published as engravings in
England in a volume called *Hudson River Portfolio*. These were the source for further
designs by the engravers, and were later used by J. & R. Clews to produce a series of
underglaze prints in various colours. The name of Bentley, Wear & Bourne, engravers
of Shelton, previously noted, appears on some designs for the American market. The
American trade in dark blue-printed wares reached its height between 1825 and 1830,
Enoch Wood producing the greatest number of designs. Andrew Stevenson, J. & R.
Clews, Joseph Stubbs, J. & W. Ridgway, Ralph Stevenson and R. Stevenson &
Williams, during their short partnership, all produced their quota, as also did a
number of smaller firms. Thomas Mayer issued an ornamental series of the arms of
American states (pl. 42).

In the 1830s there was much labour unrest at home. Ward, writing of this time,
states: 'The masters were called to encounter a formidable combination of the workmen to raise wages. The operatives, by mandate from the Union Lodge, systematically
turned out in a mass from any manufactory where their Prices and Rules were not

granted. The evil became so great at length that nearly all the manufacturers combined in their turn and completely closed their works for a period of several months. The struggle terminated early in 1837.'* In addition to these labour troubles the American trade began to dry up and, according to the same authority, by 1837 had reached a state of 'great stagnation'. There was, in fact, a financial crisis in that year in America caused by buying and borrowing to excess: stringent restrictions were imposed by the Bank of England on the discounting of American bills.† By this time many of the firms who had specialised in underglaze blue printing had gone out of business.

About 1830, potters had begun to print American views in various underglaze colours including a light blue, and those firms still in existence now began to look for fresh export outlets for their scenic transfer-printed wares. A number of foreign landscapes, French, African, Indian and especially Italian scenery began to appear. In 1828, James Keeling of Hanley introduced services decorated with views taken from the illustrations of Buckingham's *Travels in Mesopotamia*; others followed with views in Turkey, Persia and Hindustan.‡ Enoch Wood & Sons issued a set of 12 views in France. Many of these foreign scenes were copied from engravings after water colours by travelling artists: one such was William Henry Bartlett (1809–54). About 1830, he travelled on the Continent and subsequently visited Turkey, Asia Minor, Egypt and Arabia; he also paid four visits to America.

English views were still popular at home, but in addition other and more original work began to appear. J. & R. Clews (1818–34) of Cobridge issued in quick succession their Dr Syntax (pls. 19 and 20) and Don Quixote series. The former was issued in three sets, about 30 engravings in all, taken from the drawings of Thomas Rowlandson, illustrating a book by Dr William Combe as a satire upon the tours of William Gilpin (1724–1804). These were published in three volumes, *Tour in Search of the Picturesque*, *Tour in Search of Consolation* and *Tour in Search of a Wife*, between 1815 and 1821. The Don Quixote designs were reproduced from engravings by Robert Smirke, illustrating the adventures of Don Quixote de la Mancha. About 20 of these engravings have been recorded. This same firm also produced seven domestic scenes engraved after paintings by Sir David Wilkie, who had become a Royal Academician in 1811. These are all in dark blue, as opposed to the somewhat similar sentimental subjects in light blue by John Rogers & Son of Longport, such as 'The Adopted Child' and 'Love in a Village' (pl. 59). William Adams issued a number of pictures of animals (pl. 10), some based on paintings of Sir Edwin Landseer. Enoch Wood did some scriptural subjects, as did Adams, Mason, Jackson, Ridgway and others, but some of these were in colours other than blue.

There were numerous other subjects used by the transfer engravers. The coming

---

* Ward, *op. cit.*, p. 67
† J. Guiseppi, *The Bank of England*, 1966, pp. 96–7
‡ Shaw, *op. cit.*, p. 226

of the railways in the 1830s and '40s produced a few designs. To this period also belong the many rather nondescript compositions with the pattern name printed on the
back in a foliated or flowery cartouche. Smaller pieces, with illustrations of nursery
rhymes, or of a commemorative nature (pl. 113), were issued in large numbers. These
were made in Staffordshire, but to an even greater extent at centres outside the
Potteries, such as Newcastle, Sunderland and Swansea. From about 1830 the potters
were beginning to give up the rich dark blue in favour of a lighter and duller tint which
in its turn, was gradually almost entirely superseded by the cheapened process of
colour printing.

Attribution of Staffordshire Blue

LATE eighteenth-century examples of underglaze blue transfer-printed earthenware are comparatively rare. These early pieces will almost invariably be decorated with pseudo-Chinese designs. If marked, they are, with few exceptions, impressed with the name or initials of the maker. The one outstanding exception to this was the Caughley mark—Thomas Turner carried on the same practice used on his printed porcelain, where the pieces were marked with a transfer-printed open crescent, letter 'c' or 's', or occasionally with the name 'Salopian' in full. Early impressed marks which may sometimes be seen are those of Heath (pl. 31), Turner, Adams and Wolfe (pl. 75). Plates of this period were often octagonal and were sometimes edged in brown over the glaze on the rim, imitating imported Chinese porcelain. Early wares of Minton and Spode seem rarely to have been marked. A few pieces with an impressed mark 'Spode' appear to be early. The impressed mark 'SPODE', in capital letters, often accompanied by the same mark printed in blue, usually appears to be of a later date. Firms founded in the second decade of the nineteenth century, or shortly afterwards, such as R. Stevenson, J. & W. Ridgway, J. & R. Riley, A. Stevenson, J. & R. Clews and J. Stubbs, who specialised in this type of decoration at the height of its popularity, were on the whole fairly meticulous in marking a large proportion of their wares. These names frequently appear either printed or impressed and sometimes both. Marks of this period often contain the proud words 'Warranted Staffordshire'. After about 1835 marks seem to have become much less common on blue and white wares, except in the case of some well-known, long-established firms. Davenport have a particularly good record in this respect: it is unusual to find a piece from this Longport firm made after about 1800, unmarked with either a name or an anchor, or both. From the number of marked specimens met with made at factories outside the Potteries, such as Leeds, the Don and Brameld potteries at Swinton, it would appear that they marked a large proportion of their blue-printed wares. It is on record that the Committee of Management of the Herculaneum Pottery at Liverpool went so far as to pass a resolution on 6 August 1822 'to give publicity and identity to the China and Earthenware manufactured by the Herculaneum Pottery, the words HERCULANEUM POTTERY be stamped or marked on some conspicuous part of all China and Earthenware hereafter made and manufactured at this manufactory'.*

As new bodies were introduced, it became the mode to include the description such as 'stone china', 'ironstone', 'semi' or 'opaque china' in the printed mark. Sometimes the name or initials of the firm were included, but unfortunately very often not. The same remarks apply to the foliated or flowery cartouche marks, encircling the name of the pattern, which usually denote the 1830–40 period. The garter or the strap and buckle, and the Staffordshire knot, became favourite devices in which to enclose the name or initials of the maker. John & Richard Riley of Burslem were probably the first to use the former on blue-printed wares. Later, both these devices became common as part of trade marks, often omitting the name of the manufacturer. The words 'Limited', 'Trade mark' or 'England', included in a trade mark, denote a late date. The first two were never used before 1860 and 1862 respectively, and 'England' never before some time in the 1880s.

The very large number of manufacturers of blue underglaze transfer-printed earthenware makes it very difficult to attribute unmarked pieces. Occasionally the factory can be identified by the shape of the cartouche or scroll in which the name of the pattern is printed. More often it is possible to identify the maker of unmarked pieces by means of the border pattern. Although the same central view or pattern was sometimes printed by competing potters, it was unusual before 1830 for the same border design to be used by more than one potter. A few exceptions to this rule have been noted, which can usually be accounted for by the factory being sold up, or taken over, including the copper plates. Most potters used several different border patterns, and these appear to have been used almost as trade marks. Where these were supplied by engraving shops, there was probably an agreement that they would not be supplied to any other firm.

All the early borders were in keeping with the *chinoiserie* patterns, and consisted of complicated cell and diaper designs, or brocaded patterns commonly seen on Chinese and Japanese porcelain. This style was almost universal until the end of the eighteenth century. At some time between 1802 and 1805 William Brooke(s), an engraver of Tunstall, is said to have suggested to John Clive, a master potter of the same town, a method of using a continuous strip border, similar to those used with contemporary wallpaper hangings. This innovation was soon adopted by all potters, and was the origin of the familiar repeat patterns, which were subsequently issued in extraordinarily diverse variations. Except for the still-popular Willow and similar oriental patterns the old-type border was completely superseded.

Some of these early borders used the device of incorporating small vignettes decorated with sketches relevant to the main design. An example of this can be seen on some pieces in the style of Claude, said to have been engraved by William Brooke(s)

* Mayer, *op. cit.*, p. 88

for Benjamin Adams; reserves at regular intervals contain Grecian buildings. Spode favoured this type of border on some of his Italianate series. In the same mode, the borders of his Indian Sporting services were continuous repeat patterns of birds and animals in their natural surroundings (pl. 62). J. & R. Clews and other potters used this style at a later date. Some of the patterns made for the American market had well-executed portraits of American celebrities placed in varying arrangements around the rims.

An early border used by William Adams of Stoke on his English views consisted of framing the distant scene with an irregular mass of foliage of trees, and herbage in the foreground, encroaching into the well of the plate or dish. He used this type of border in two forms; on country scenes, with a wide scroll edge on the rim of the piece (pl. 6), and on London views without the scroll edge (pl. 5). A similar type of border was used by the little-known firm of Tams & Co. and appears on all of his very few recorded scenic views, both British (pls. 70 and 71) and American. Other Adams borders are various arrangements of foliage and flowers, one with bell- and chrysanthemum type flowers (pl. 8), another with large flowers and fruit covering much of the centre as well as the rim of the piece.

The earliest American scenes made by Enoch Wood date from the time when the style of the firm was Wood & Caldwell, and were enclosed in a plain border of flowers (pl. 76). This partnership came to an end in 1818 when the firm became Enoch Wood & Sons. It was probably about this time that they introduced a very striking border made up of a conventional arrangement of sea-shells, and seaweed. There were two versions of this design, one with, and the other without, a prominent cockle shell (pl. 80). These appear on both English and American views. Another potter to use a shell border was Rogers; these have only been recorded on shipping scenes (pl. 56). Enoch Wood also used a very attractive grape-vine with fruit design on his British scenes. The 'London Views' of this series appear in an attractive frame with the border pattern extended to overlap the central medallion (pl. 77). All the other views, outside London, take up the entire centre of the piece (pl. 78). Many other border designs were used by this manufactory before they ceased production in 1846. A late set of about 20 'English Cities', issued in light blue and other colours, has a broad border of medallions, scrolls and flowers reminiscent of some of the early brocaded patterns. Several Italian views were issued, surrounded by a broad design of flying cupids, flowers and foliage. The Don Pottery at Swinton also issued Italian scenes with a similar type of border (pl. 101).

J. & R. Clews (1818–34) mostly favoured border designs made up of different arrangements of flowers and scrolls. These appeared on some of their American views, and in various forms for the Syntax (pl. 20) and Wilkie services. The Don Quixote designs were framed in a flower border with a bird perched at the top of the pattern, and a peculiar scallop of beading threading its way around the whole picture. Other borders were arrangements of flowers and leaves, usually large: one with lily- and camellia-type flowers used on some of their English scenes is especially attractive (pl. 18). Another flower border, found on some of their other English views, is exactly the same as the bell- and chrysanthemum-type flower pattern already mentioned as used by William Adams (pl. 8). This is one of the rare cases of the same early border being used by two potters.

J. & W. Ridgway (1814–30) used a rather stiff border of conventional medallions of roses. This appears on all their American views. Their series of colleges and important buildings in Oxford and Cambridge is bordered with a trailing convolvulus, quartered by medallions of cherubs feeding and milking goats. This series can be numbered among the examples which demonstrate the underglaze printing technique at its height (pl. 50). The Herculaneum Pottery at Liverpool produced views of Oxford and Cambridge, among their series of the principal towns in England, on which a similar border device was used; the floral border was broken by medallions of boys with a classical vase (pl. 110). The same border was used on a series of more general, named views (pl. 111). When the two Ridgway brothers separated in 1830, each produced some views in light blue with rather dreary borders: John used a design of large and small, five-pointed stars, William various arrangements of moss.

Ralph Stevenson (1810–32) of Cobridge used various borders of foliage and flowers. One of vine leaves alone was used on American views. His most distinctive border is one of oak leaves and acorns.* This was used on both English and American scenes, and was also used during his short partnership with Williams (pl. 65). Several American pictures were produced marked with the names in full, or the initials R.S.W.

Andrew Stevenson (1816–30), also of Cobridge, used different designs of scrolls, leaves and flowers, notably roses, but nothing very outstanding. His pieces are marked with the impressed name; the impressed 'ship' mark (pl. 64) formerly ascribed to Ralph Stevenson is now held by most authorities to belong to Andrew.†

Joseph Stubbs (1822–35) used a border of foliage and pointed scrolls on his English views. On his American pieces he introduced three or four equidistant eagles between the scrolls (pl. 66). The eagle, naturally enough, became a popular emblem with the potters who competed for the American market, both on the front of their wares as decoration, or on the back as part of the mark. Impressed or printed eagles became part of many marks on earthenwares made for both the home and export trade.

One noteworthy border is that of Thomas Mayer of Stoke. He exported extensively to America, and on all his borders he introduced into the pattern a wheel-like device at intervals, three on plates, and four on dishes (pl. 42).

Some of the early wares had pierced and embossed borders instead of the usual plain rim. Turner, Benjamin Adams and Davenport often used this style, and were followed by a few of the later potters. After about 1835 border designs tended to

---

* This border has been reproduced on a series of historic American subjects in the twentieth century

† J. Arnold Fleming in *Scottish Pottery*, 1923, attributes this mark to James Stevenson & Co. of Greenock (*q.v.*)

become less distinctive, and much of the individuality disappeared. The great majority were rather monotonous stereotyped flower and leaf designs. By the middle of the century there was a general deterioration in the standard of printing. Transfer papers were often applied carelessly, when it is possible to see the joins where patterns do not meet properly, although this fault is not always absent in earlier pieces.

It is rarely possible to date pieces exactly. Some patterns remained in use over a long period and very few documentary, dated pieces exist. The colour of the blue used can be no more than a very rough guide in helping to date specimens. During the course of its history, blue-printed ware has been produced in every conceivable shade, varying from a very light to a very dark, sometimes almost purple blue. At all times there were wide variations in the colour used by the different potters, and many of them used a light and dark blue at the same time. Maintaining a uniform colour depended on the purity of the cobalt used, the control of the firing temperature in the kiln, and the skill of the craftsmen employed. The early prints of Thomas Turner and his contemporaries were always in a strong, deep, but rather dull blue, as they lacked the fine glass-like qualities of the later glazes to bring out their full colour. As engraving technique and the qualities of the bodies and glazes improved, a softer, richer tone was obtained. Spode may have been the first to produce a good pale blue, at some time at the end of the eighteenth century. What is now known as 'Spode blue' varies from a very faint to a rather deeper shade, covered with a soft smooth glaze. This colour remained fashionable until about 1815, when a heavy, dark, intense blue was introduced. Some authorities attribute this innovation to Enoch Wood, others to William Adams of Stoke. This colour appears to have made a greater appeal in America, and was soon adopted by many potters. The lighter blue began to come back into general use about 1830, at the time when underglaze colours other than blue were becoming fashionable.

Final attribution of unmarked pieces which cannot be identified by any of the means already mentioned must usually be delayed until a marked piece is discovered. Sometimes, even if a name or initials are included in a mark, it is not always possible to identify the maker, if the name has not been recorded, or the initials can be applicable to more than one factory. In the latter case an approximation in dating can sometimes be a help in attribution. This can often be done by an assessment of the type of body, the shape, the engraved pattern and border design, occasionally the colour, and even the type of mark itself.

Marks

IT is always satisfying to a collector to be able to identify the maker of a piece of pottery, however attractive and interesting it may be without this knowledge. But so many potters made blue-printed earthenware during the 70 years under review that, even after a great deal of research, it is usually difficult, and often impossible, to determine the manufacturer, unless a piece is clearly marked. Various aids to identification have been discussed in the chapter on 'Attribution of Staffordshire Blue'.

Some of the later potters, and perhaps some of the earlier, lesser-known ones, seem to have made a point of not marking their wares, possibly in order to be able to compete more easily with better-known makers. Cases even occur where firms deliberately used misleading marks, hoping that they would be mistaken for those of an old-established, more reputable potter. Others, however meticulous they may have been in applying marks, were accustomed to marking only a certain number of pieces in each service, obviously never dreaming that individual pieces might one day be sought by collectors.

In the case of impressed marks, these had to be applied to the ware before the first firing, and, in the early days, were nearly always the plain name-mark of the potter or firm. This type of mark was used almost universally on blue-printed earthenwares in the last two decades of the eighteenth century, a notable exception being Thomas Turner of Caughley. In the nineteenth century, when underglaze printing on earthenwares was fully established, the practice of using printed marks was quickly developed. Impressed marks were still largely used, but these were often accompanied by a further printed mark.

Josiah Spode II probably initiated the practice of printing the title of the engraving on the bottom of his pieces (fig. 57). The use of ornamental scrolls for this purpose soon followed (figs. 4 and 69). Enoch Wood and William Adams began to use this device in the second decade of the nineteenth century. This developed into the foliated and flowery cartouche and wreath marks which became almost universal with printed marks (figs. 7 and 25) and which reached their height in the 1830–40 period. Minton used a great many different patterns of this type of mark to contain the name of the pattern, or the type of earthenware body, but in addition they nearly always included the initials of the current partnership: many potters omitted this last information. The practice of using a printed cartouche mark, containing the description of the type of body only, became a very common one. Swansea used several different ones for their opaque china (figs. 91 and 92) without including a factory mark.

Impressed letters and numbers were usually tally marks used by the workmen: this also applies to the majority of printed marks of this type. A few impressed single letters have been attributed to specific potters by some authorities e.g. D for Dillwyn, S for Shorthose or W for Wood, but these have to be treated with caution. Single letters as part of a printed pattern mark are more reliable. Thomas Dimmock used the letter D in this type of mark. B has been noted on a printed mark on a piece also bearing the impressed stamp BRAMELD. But these single letters usually fit many potters, and without further evidence it is dangerous to be dogmatic. Some workmen's marks are peculiar to a particular factory and can, therefore, be treated almost as a factory mark. An example of this are the club, diamond, heart and spade-like devices, either painted or impressed, used at Swansea (fig. 93), although the spade-like mark has also been recorded on some Leeds ware. A cross within a circle (fig. 58) is given by some authorities as a Spode mark. This certainly appeared on some early Spode porcelain and was occasionally used on blue-printed earthenwares.

Potters occasionally adopted a sign or device with their marks. The mark ROGERS sometimes appears with the sign for Iron or Mars (fig. 53), so that pieces bearing this mark alone are usually attributed to that pottery. An arrow with or without the letter S (figs. 54 and 55) is attributed by some authorities to Shorthose of Hanley. An anchor was used by several potters. Davenport, T. & J. Carey, T. Fell, the Herculaneum Pottery at Liverpool, and the Middlesbrough Pottery included this device in some of their marks: appearing alone without a name it relates, more often than not, to Davenport. The Belle Vue Pottery, Hull, used a mark which included two bells (figs. 73 and 74) and sometimes appears without the name of the pottery. The firm J. & M. P. Bell & Co. of Glasgow used a single bell as a mark (fig. 75), but this was not until after 1842. Similarly the Herculaneum Pottery, when the firm was Case & Mort, introduced in 1833 a mark of a Liver bird (figs. 85 and 86), either impressed or printed, which sometimes appears without any other distinguishing mark.

Seal marks in imitation of those used on Chinese wares have often been used by English potters. They are frequently seen on eighteenth century red wares. An early nineteenth-century seal mark with an R in the centre is attributed to Job Ridgway (fig. 47). Spode frequently used this type of mark after 1810 but these always bore the name SPODE (fig. 56). Other seal marks, usually with what appear to be disguised letters in them, are attributed to the Meigh firm of Hanley. Miles Mason used a seal mark with or without his name (figs. 36 and 37).

The Royal Arms, the Prince of Wales' feather crest, and Crowns occur in many marks, usually with the name of the potter. But there were exceptions. Both Hicks & Meigh and Hicks, Meigh & Johnson used the pre-Victorian version of the Royal Arms with STONE CHINA and a number below, but without the name of the firm (fig. 30). The latter partnership also used a crown within a wreath, either with or without the title of the firm (fig. 31). At a later date Samuel Alcock used the Victorian version of the Royal Arms, usually labelled S. A. & Co., but sometimes without. John Ridgway and John Ridgway & Co. also on occasions used both the printed Royal Arms and Crown marks without their names or initials (figs. 106 and 107). An impressed crown with no other marking is attributed to the Middlesbrough Pottery, but other potters almost certainly used this mark too. When Turner & Abbott were appointed potters to the Prince of Wales in 1784, the feather crest was used with the name TURNER, either printed or impressed (fig. 67). The same crest has been recorded with the initials J. D. B. relating to John Denton Baxter of Hanley who was working in the 1820s. C. Heathcote & Co. were another firm to use this crest (figs. 28 and 29).

The eagle was adopted as a mark by many potters competing for the American market. Adams, Mayer, Wood and many others used this as part of their impressed and printed marks (figs. 1, 3 and 94). Occasionally an impressed or printed eagle appears alone, to set another problem for the collector.

The Staffordshire knot and the garter or strap and buckle marks made their appearance in the 1820s. The latter was probably used first by the Rileys (fig. 44) always with a name. Later many potters used this device as part of their mark, but often omitted their name. At first the Staffordshire knot appeared as part of a mark, but later became a favourite vehicle for containing the initials of the firm within the loops (figs. 15 and 104).

Many attractive blue-printed patterns may be found on earthenwares with no mark other than a printed scroll or cartouche containing the title or view-name of the design. If these are not by the better-known potters whose border patterns or cartouche shaped marks can be recognised, one hopes that another piece will eventually turn up which is marked with the potter's name. Too often, however, pieces found subsequently bear exactly the same mark and still no indication of the manufacturer. Even more frustrating is when a specimen does turn up with a name or initial mark which still cannot be identified. A typical case of this occurred with a platter, one of an interesting series called 'Metropolitan Scenery' with such titles as 'North End, Hampstead' (pl. 83) and 'Windsor Castle', the latter with a game of cricket being played in the foreground. They appear to be of the 1820–40 period with an attractive floral border, the passion flower being predominant. Eventually a piece was found with the same printed mark (fig. 97) and the very clearly impressed initials G. C., which do not appear to relate to any of the recorded potters. The Staffordshire knot included in the mark shows that the series is of Staffordshire origin. It is tempting to interpret the impressed mark as Ginder & Co. or even Godwin of Cobridge, but this is not very convincing. Doubtless further evidence will become available which will give the correct solution.

Two different views of Richmond, Surrey, a beauty spot which was a favourite subject with artists and potters of this period, are illustrated (pls. 86 and 87). These platters, despite having been in their owners' possession for 30 years, remain un-attributed. With their distinctive border patterns and cartouche and scroll view-name marks (figs. 95 and 96) this should, in theory, not be difficult. There can be little doubt that marked specimens exist with one of these distinguishing features which would give the answer. Many such problem pieces (in these cases perhaps only to the author) exist which, with time and patience and co-operation amongst collectors, can event-ually be correctly attributed (pls. 88–91, 116–19).

A pertinent example of a potter the greater part of whose blue-printed wares has remained anonymous until now is Henshall & Co. (*q.v.*). He issued a set of American views including the Court House and the Exchange, both in Baltimore, and the Dam and Waterworks at Philadelphia. He also issued a set of English views, including one of York Minster (pl. 33). Both series are well-designed, in a medium dark blue with an attractive border of fruit and flowers. No mark on these pieces has yet been noticed, other than a floral cartouche containing the name of the view. Any illustrations have always been described as 'maker unknown'. Now an example of another series called 'British Views' (pl. 34) in the same cartouche (fig. 27) and the same fruit and flower border has turned up with the very rare impressed mark HENSHALL & CO. All these series can now be safely attributed to this firm and add another name to those who can be considered to rank among the leading makers of blue-printed wares.

List of Earthenware Potters, 1780–1850

SUITABLE kilns for the manufacture of pots to supply the needs of the neighbourhood sprang up in the Middle Ages in many parts of the country, wherever there were suitable beds of clay. Those in Staffordshire first received special notice when Dr Robert Plot wrote his *Natural History of Staffordshire* published in 1686, in which he names Burslem as the principal centre of manufacture. Later, when the supply of wood fuel became rare and costly, and a higher technical standard was demanded, many potters were forced out of existence. Those in Staffordshire, having an alternative supply of fuel in coal, were able to survive. A cluster of hamlets, parishes and townships in North Staffordshire became known as 'The Potteries' and are now amalgamated to form the County Borough of Stoke-on-Trent.

This centre of the ceramic industry with its steady progress in all branches of the art gradually attained a position unique in Europe, and indeed throughout the world. The development of the cream-coloured, and then the white earthenware, bodies finally established the position of the Potteries in world markets and made possible the enormous output of underglaze blue transfer-printed wares.

The following alphabetical list of earthenware potters of the relevant period, with short biographical details where available, includes as many as possible of those of whom records have survived. Following the list of Staffordshire potters are the other contemporary centres of pottery manufacture. These were usually situated around ports, where clay and coal could be easily and cheaply supplied, or at places which had their own local supply of clay and coal available.

It is not, of course, claimed that all these potters made underglaze blue-printed wares; but it seems reasonable to suppose that any of them making general earthenwares for any length of time during this period could ill afford not to use this method of decoration at some time or other. What is much more certain is that there were other short-lived manufacturers of this type of pottery, of whom all records have disappeared.

In compiling these notes on early potters a great deal of use has been made of the books by the first ceramic historians, namely Shaw, Ward and Jewitt. It must be remembered, however, that it took some years to gather the information contained in these books, and firms listed in them may in some cases have ceased to exist before the date of publication. Other specialist books by modern writers have been consulted in addition to many 'mark' books, the most recent of which, the *Encyclopaedia of British Pottery and Porcelain Marks,** is quite outstanding, and invaluable as a guide to marks of pottery and porcelain manufacturers up to the present day. It also includes many previously unrecorded potters of earlier days.

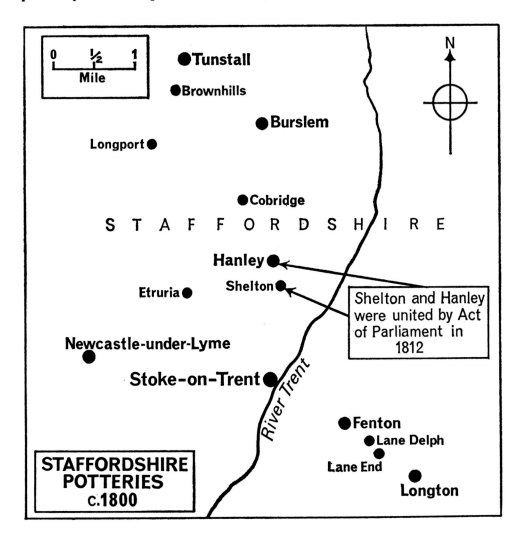

* Geoffrey A. Godden, published in 1964 by Herbert Jenkins Ltd.

Factories have been subdivided as follows:

1 Staffordshire potteries
2 West Country potteries—Bristol, Swansea and district
3 Shropshire—Caughley and district
4 Derbyshire—Chesterfield, Burton-on-Trent, Swadlincote
5 Yorkshire—Leeds and district, Swinton and district, Middlesbrough, Hull and district
6 Lancashire—Liverpool and district
7 Durham—Sunderland and district
8 Northumberland—Newcastle-upon-Tyne and district
9 Scotland
10 Supplementary list

Abbott, Andrew Whether Abbott was a potter in his own right before he became a partner of John Turner of Lane End, as Turner & Abbott (*q.v.*) about 1781 is uncertain. In that year he appears to have joined Turner as his London partner in charge of the warehouse in Old Fish Street. In 1782 they moved their showrooms to Fleet Street and opened a decorating establishment in addition. John Turner died in December 1787, but Abbott continued his London partnership with the sons, William and John, until they withdrew in 1792.

Abbott & Newbury Abbott retained the Fleet Street premises and took a man named Newbury into partnership and acted as London agent for several potters, including the Turners. They also bought wares in the white for decoration to their own design.

Abbott & Mist In 1802 Abbott dissolved the partnership with Newbury and took James Underhill Mist as his new partner, an arrangement which continued until Abbott retired in 1811.

Mist, James Mist leased the Fleet Street premises from Abbott and remained in business on his own until about 1814.

ABBOTT & MIST marks have been recorded, and also that of J. MIST. An impressed mark _{MIST SOLE AGENT} TURNER appearing on a blue-printed Willow pattern plate has been recorded by Bevis Hillier.*

Adams An important group of master potters who share with Spode the distinction of being the best-known and most written-about family, after Wedgwood, in the history of Staffordshire earthenwares, and perhaps the most important in the manufacture of 'blue-printed'. Their story begins, so far as underglaze transfer-printing is concerned, with three cousins, all named William Adams.

Adams, William of Brick House, Burslem, and Cobridge. His father died when
1748–1831   he was only nine years of age, and the family pottery at Brick House Works, Burslem, was let to Josiah Wedgwood until 1773. William Adams had started a new factory at Sneyd Green, Cobridge in 1770, and for some time after 1773 ran the Burslem and Cobridge works in conjunction. After a few years he again let

* B. Hillier, *Master Potters of the Industrial Revolution. The Turners of Lane End*, 1965, p. 30, pl. 24b

the Burslem works and transferred all his business to Cobridge, where he was interested in several potteries, including one in partnership with his step-father, conducted as Hales & Adams (*q.v.*).

At Cobridge, in 1775, Adams engaged William Davis, who had gained experience in printing at both Worcester and Caughley. After making experiments in overglaze and glue-bat printing, he is said to have been successful in underglaze blue printing at an early date after 1780, and the first to introduce it into Staffordshire. His obituary notice in the *Monthly Magazine* for March 1831 noted that 'he was formerly a manufacturer of earthenware, and one of the earliest introducers of blue printing in the manufacture'.* His earliest designs would have been of conventional oriental subjects but difficult to identify, as few, if any, appear to have been marked. Very little of the history of the Cobridge factory is recorded. William Adams had many interests outside potting, and his three sons, none of whom survived their father by very long, all died without issue. He gave up manufacturing some years before his death in 1831. He is known to have let one pottery in Cobridge in 1813 and another one to J. & R. Clews in 1817.

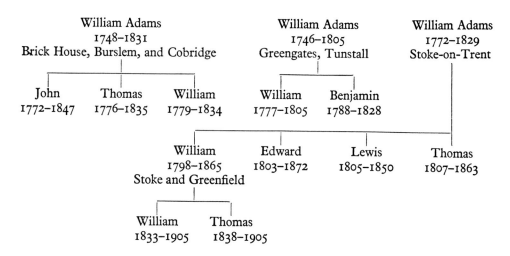

Adams, William   of Greengates, Tunstall, was a close friend and rival of Josiah
1746–1805   Wedgwood. He is known more particularly for his jasper and stonewares in the Wedgwood tradition, but unlike Wedgwood he took considerable interest in the possibilities of underglaze printing. He started potting at a small factory in Burslem, which he gave up when he built larger works at Greengates, Tunstall, about 1780. With knowledge probably acquired from his Cobridge cousin he is said to have produced the first blue-printed in Tunstall about 1787, and by 1790 was turning out quite large quantities. Pieces attributed to him are light in weight

* W. Turner, *William Adams, an Old English Potter*, 1923, p. 194

and well engraved in an attractive tint of blue. They are the usual Willow and other oriental style of patterns, and in the same shapes as the popular creamware, such as sweetmeat trays, supper dishes and covers (pl. 3). If marked, they have the impressed mark ADAMS. William Adams died in 1805 and, his eldest son William having died in the same year, the factory was carried on by trustees until his youngest son, Benjamin, came of age in 1809.

Adams, Benjamin of Greengates, Tunstall, continued to make blue-printed wares
   1788–1828 in large quantities, first on pearl ware and later on stone china, all in pale or medium blue. They were similar in type to those of his father, and pieces such as heart-shaped dishes, salad bowls, pickle trays, fruit baskets and bowls may still be seen; plates often have pierced borders (pl. 4). Marked pieces have the impressed stamp B. ADAMS, and this probably indicates the period from 1809, when he came of age, to the closing of the factory in 1820.

 William Brooke(s) is said to have executed many engravings for the Greengates factory, including one well-known pattern after Claude Lorraine (pl. 4). Bad health, and perhaps lack of interest, added to heavy losses with unfortunate exports forced Benjamin Adams to sell the works in 1820.

Adams, William of Stoke-on-Trent learnt his potting with Lewis Heath of the
   1772–1829 Hadderidge manufactory at Burslem and was a partner in that firm from 1793 until 1804. In that year he took over the Cliff Bank Works at Stoke, and this is the important factory and period so far as collectors of blue-printed are concerned. He traded as William Adams until he took his sons into partnership, first William in 1819, and later Edward, Lewis and Thomas, when the style of the firm became William Adams & Sons.

Adams, William & Sons The firm had extended enormously by 1818, when it had five separate potteries in Stoke. William Adams died in 1829, and his eldest son William (1798–1865) became senior partner, but the style of the firm remained unchanged as William Adams & Sons until the Stoke factories were closed in 1863. In 1834 the Greenfield factory, acquired on marriage by William, the new head of the business, was added to the firm. In 1853, owing to ill health, he severed his connection with Stoke, retaining only the Greenfield factory for himself. Lewis having died in 1850, the Stoke factories were carried on by Edward and Thomas. Edward took little part in the management, and the works at Stoke were closed in 1863 on the death of Thomas. The Greenfield factory was continued by William's two sons after his death in 1865.

 William Adams (1772–1829) must have had experience in making blue-printed earthenwares during his partnership with Lewis Heath at Burslem. When he started at Stoke in 1804 he soon produced a large variety of wares of which blue-printed became a very considerable part. In addition to the Willow pattern and other oriental designs, he used a whole range of rustic, sentimental and classical scenes (pl. 9). The engravings for which he is best known are views of London buildings, which included the Bank of England and St Paul's School, but are mainly different views in Regent's Park, and a large selection of important buildings and country houses throughout Britain. These began to appear about 1815 and were issued in the new rich dark blue, and probably remained popular until about 1830. The London views seem to have invariably had the tree and foliage border (pl. 5) already described; some of the country scenes were enclosed in a similar type of border of a different design with a scroll edging round the rim of the piece (pl. 7).* Other country scenes, mainly castles and abbeys, had a border of bell- and chrysanthemum-type flowers (pl. 8), also used by Clews. Yet another series, mostly of stately homes, had an attractive border pattern of large flowers, leaves and scrolls. A very rare border, only occasionally seen and appearing on a view of Whitby Harbour, consists of an arrangement of fruit and flowers, covering much of the centre of the piece as well as the rim.

In addition to a large home market, the firm worked up a tremendous business in exports. In 1821 William Adams (1798–1865) went to America and opened offices in New York. He returned home two years later, bringing many American designs with him. It is remarkable that the only recorded American scene in dark blue is one of Mitchell & Freeman's China and Glass Warehouse, Chatham Street, Boston. It seems that these designs were not used until later, when American views were issued in the 1830s, in various colours, mainly pink and green, and only a very few in light blue. These, as well as the usual topographical pictures, included the 'Columbus and Indian' series. About 1830 his younger brother, Thomas, opened offices in Mexico, and a large trade followed with that country and Cuba and Brazil: a Spanish series was produced for these countries (pl. 11); the 'Athens' and 'Bologna' patterns were also well received and remained in vogue for many years. Other late designs, issued in light and medium blue, were views in Palestine, India and France. Among other engravings were scriptural subjects, and a set of animal pictures (pl. 10), some of the latter based on paintings by Sir Edwin Landseer, issued in the 1830s.

Many of the scenic views bear both an impressed and a printed mark. The impressed mark on dark blue transfers is usually circular, with a crown or an eagle surrounded by the words ADAMS WARRANTED STAFFORDSHIRE (figs. 1 and 2). The eagle appears to be the most usual mark but the eagle and the crown appear on both London and country views, and may possibly signify that they were intended for either the American or the home market. The printed mark on London views is always an eagle with outstretched wings with the name of the scene on a festooned ribbon (fig. 3). The name of country views may be on any one of several decorative scrolls (figs. 4 to 7). Later pieces are often stamped ADAMS or W. ADAMS.

W. ADAMS & SONS or W.A. & S. appear on some printed marks.

* In these cases the name of the view always seems to be omitted

Adams & Prince of Lane Delph, Fenton. A rare impressed mark occasionally found on earthenwares. One authority gives the date as c. 1810, another as late eighteenth or early nineteenth century. Jewitt gives the date as about 1760. Shaw states that 'John Adams and John Prince were manufacturers at Lane Delph, near Fenton Lane, of red porcelain, and white stone ware, salt glaze'.* This appears to point to a date well before the end of the eighteenth century and it is unlikely therefore that the mark would turn up on any blue-printed ware.

Alcock, John & George of Cobridge, manufacturers of earthenwares listed by Ward in 1843. The *Encyclopaedia of British Pottery and Porcelain Marks* gives the dates as 1839–46. The impressed or printed marks are the initials J. & G.A. or J. & G. ALCOCK COBRIDGE sometimes including the name of the body and/or the name of the pattern.

They were succeeded by John & Samuel Alcock, Junior.

Alcock, Samuel & Co. took over the Hill Works, Burslem from John & Richard Riley soon after they gave up in 1828. According to Jewitt the firm was Alcock & Keeling for a short time before Keeling retired, when the firm became S. Alcock & Co. The works were rebuilt and much enlarged in 1839. Ward states that in 1842 they were next in importance to Enoch Wood & Sons in Burslem and shared with them a very large export trade to America. The Hill Pottery was sold in 1860. This firm had another factory at Cobridge presumed to have started about 1828, about the same time as Burslem. Shaw notes their presence in Cobridge in 1829, without comment. They made many types of earthenware, including blue-printed. If marked, their wares bear the impressed or printed name or initials. The mark sometimes includes the Royal Arms with or without the initials; another mark shows a beehive surrounded by foliage with a scroll underneath with the name of the firm.

Allerton, Brough & Green of Park Works, Lane End, Longton, are listed in Ward's list of 1841 Longton potters. According to Jewitt, this firm was established in 1831. In 1859 the firm became Charles Allerton & Sons, who made large quantities of blue-printed wares, but are too late to be of much interest.

Astbury Several plates of a pearl ware-type body painted with *chinoiseries* in underglaze blue bear the impressed name ASTBURY. These appear to be of the 1780–90 period, and the same potter could presumably have used underglaze blue printing, although no examples have yet been recorded. This mark probably refers to Richard Meir Astbury, recorded as potting between Lane End and Lane Delph about 1790–1800. The impressed initials R.M.A. have also been noted.

* Shaw, *op. cit.*, p. 175

Aynsley, John of Lane End was a practical potter, engraver and decorator of earthenwares. He was established at a pottery in Lane End about 1780, and died in 1826. He is best known for his signed, black overglaze prints, on cream-coloured and white wares, much of which appear to have been made by other manufacturers. His engravings may well have been used for underglaze printing, but no marked prints have yet been recorded.

Baddeleys of Shelton. The history of the Baddeley family is somewhat confusing. John Baddeley, an old-established potter, had died in 1771 leaving four sons Ralph, John, Thomas and Edward. Most early reference books state that John and Edward Baddeley were the successors of Ralph and John, but this is clearly wrong. It now appears probable that Ralph inherited a pottery from his father which he operated on his own, and his two younger brothers, John and Edward, who were under age, set up as partners at an adjoining pottery in 1784. Both firms took an early interest in blue printing.

Baddeley, Ralph of Shelton is stated by Shaw to have employed Harry Baker about 1777 to practise the method of printing with glue-bats* and later, with the help of William Smith, an engraver from Liverpool, and Thomas Davis, a printer from Worcester, he attempted the new underglaze blue-printing technique on earthenware. After many failures, he is said to have achieved complete success about 1782. Ralph Baddeley died in 1812, but had retired from the pottery business about 1800. No marked pieces appear to have been recorded.

Baddeley, John & Edward of Shelton began potting in 1784 in a factory adjacent to that of their brother Ralph and appear in the 1786 directory of Shelton potters. They retired in 1806 and the pottery was later added to that of Hicks & Meigh (*q.v.*) who in that year had commenced business in the factory previously owned by Ralph Baddeley. Shaw writes that John Baddeley engaged Thomas Radford (*q.v.*) who had been employed at Derby 'to print Tea Services by an improved method of transferring the impression to the bisquet ware'.† Wares are recorded with the impressed mark I.E.B. and, if found on blue-printed pieces, could fairly confidently be attributed to J. & E. Baddeley. An impressed B also appears on some of the pieces of the same services.

Baddeley, Thomas of Hanley. This name appears in the 1802 list as engraver and black printer of Chapel Field, Hanley. The *Encyclopaedia of British Pottery and Porcelain Marks* gives his dates as 1800–34.

Baddeley, William of Eastwood, Hanley, appears in the 1802 and 1818 lists of Hanley earthenware potters and is chiefly known for his Wedgwood-type wares. His

* Shaw, *op. cit.*, p. 212
† Shaw, *op. cit.*, p. 213

mark was EASTWOOD in capital or lower-case letters, probably in order to distinguish his wares from those of J. & E. Baddeley. As the EAST is sometimes indistinct, Jewitt surmised that this was done deliberately in order to be mistaken for Wedgwood.

Baggaley   Several potters of this name, variously spelt, are recorded as working in the Potteries in the early nineteenth century.

Baggaley, Thomas   of Tunstall is listed in the 1802 directory and the same name appears in Lane Delph in 1818.

Baggerley & Ball   of Longton, makers of earthenwares from 1822–36, who produced large quantities of blue-printed. Marks B & B or B & B/L (fig. 14).

Baggaley & Vodrey   of Tunstall were makers of blue-printed and general earthenwares about 1810. This firm may have been started by Abraham Baggaley of Golden Hill, Tunstall, who appears in the 1802 list. The partnership was probably ended some time after 1810, as in the 1818 directory an entry shows Daniel Vawdry of Golden Hill, Tunstall, a variation in spelling commonly found in these early directories.

Bagshaw & Maier (or Meir)   of Burslem. This firm apparently started as Bagshaw, Taylor & Maier in Burslem about 1798. In 1802 they are listed as Bagshaw & Maier, and continued until 1808. Mark B & M, printed or impressed.

Bailey & Batkin   of Lane End, Longton, commenced potting about 1810. Shaw states that William Bailey and his partner W. Batkin were 'one of the first who made lustre pottery',[*] and most of their wares appear to be of this type. Underglaze printed marks B. & B. occur, but possibly refer to other makers with the same initials. By 1829 Shaw refers to the firm as Bailey & Co.

Baker, W. & Co.   of Fenton—*see* Bourne & Baker.

Barker, John, William & Richard   of Lane End, were three brothers who were established in an old family pottery in 1786 as makers of creamwares, china glaze and blue wares. Richard Barker alone appears in the 1802 list, but in 1818 the firm is listed as R. J. & J. Barker of Flint Street, Lane End. Blue-printed wares with the impressed mark BARKER are recorded.

Barker, Sutton & Till   of Burslem. About 1832 this firm took the Sytch Pottery,
Barker & Till   Liverpool Road, Burslem, as successors to John Hall (*q.v.*)
Till, T.   and was still listed under these same names in Ward's list of 1843. Soon after this date until 1850 the style of the firm was Barker & Till, when it

[*] Shaw, *op. cit.*, p. 76

passed into the hands of Thomas Till. During the whole period, this pottery made general earthenwares, including blue-printed. The marks are impressed or printed, usually with the initials of the firm, sometimes with the name of the pattern added: B.S. & T., B. & T., T. TILL and later still TILL & SON.

Barlow, James & Co.   James Barlow & Co. are quoted by one authority as
Barlow & Hammersley   operating in Hanley c. 1822–39. This is probably the same firm which, elsewhere, is spoken of as Barlow & Hammersley of Hanley c. 1820. Ward in 1843 mentions this firm when listing the existing firms at that date as 'George Lomas, china factory, late Barlow & Hammersley'.

Bathwell & Goodfellow   of Burslem and Tunstall. A partnership which existed for a few years only, with two factories, one at Burslem and the other at Tunstall. Perhaps two potteries appearing in the 1802 list, Riles & Bathwell of Tunstall, and Read & Goodfellow of Burslem, were the origin of the firm. In 1818 two firms are registered in Burslem, T. & E. Bathwell of Chapel Bank, and Goodfellow & Bathwell of Upper House Works. A few years later Thomas Goodfellow (*q.v.*) took over the Phoenix Works, Tunstall. The *Encyclopaedia of British Pottery and Porcelain Marks* gives the dates of the Bathwell & Goodfellow partnership as: Burslem 1818–23; Tunstall 1820–2.

BATHWELL &
GOODFELLOW   appears as an impressed mark on printed wares.

Batkin, Walker & Broadhurst   of Lane End, makers of general earthenwares and stone china, are mentioned by Ward in his 1843 list.

The *Encyclopaedia of British Pottery and Porcelain Marks* gives the mark as B.W. & B., which appears on several printed marks of varying design, and the dates as 1840–5.

Baxter, John Denton   of High Street, Hanley, made earthenwares in the 1820s. Printed and impressed marks are BAXTER, I.D.B. or J.D.B., sometimes with the Staffordshire knot or the Prince of Wales feather crest. Blue-printed wares have been recorded.

Beardmore & Birks   *see* Griffiths, Beardmore & Birks.

Beech, James   of Tunstall. In 1821 James Beech is said to have been in partnership at the Lion Works, Sandyford, Tunstall, with Abraham Lowndes. The style of the firm in that year, according to the directory, was 'Lownds & Beech', earthenware manufacturers. Shaw mentions the firm in 1829 as Beech & Lowndes. The latter retired in 1834, when the factory was carried on by Beech alone until about 1845. The initials J.B. appear on certain American designs, notably the 'Texan Campaign' printed in blue or pink, and may refer to this firm.

Beech, William   of Burslem—*see* Jones & Beech.

Bentley, Wear & Bourne   of Vine Street, Shelton, were an important firm of en-
Bentley & Wear   gravers, printers and decorators, already noted in the
text. The style of the firm was as above from 1815–23, and Bentley & Wear from 1823–
1833. They executed many engravings for the blue-printed trade, on some of which
the name of the firm appears (pl. 39).

Birch, Edmund John   of Hanley appears on the 1802 list of potters. He is said to
have been in partnership with one of the Whitehead family of potters before he began
potting on his own from about 1796 until 1814. He is best known for his Wedgwood-
type wares, basaltes, creamwares etc. He is said to have produced blue wares, which
should refer to printed rather than painted wares at this time. He marked his wares
BIRCH or E.I.B. Jewitt states that he was succeeded at the Albion Works, Hanley by
Christopher Whitehead: this is probably an error for Charles Whitehead.

Blackwell, John & Andrew   of Cobridge appear in the directory of 1802. They
were probably the successors of Joseph & John Blackwell, who are listed separately as
earthenware potters in Cobridge in 1786. John and Andrew Blackwell made general
earthenwares, including blue-printed. In 1818 the entry appears as J. & R. Blackwell.

Boden, John   of Tunstall was a maker of earthenwares who appears in the 1818
directory, and was, according to Shaw, still a potter of note in 1829.

Boon, Edward   is listed as a Fenton potter in 1786 making Queen's Ware and
blue-painted.

Boon, Joseph   of Hanley was an established earthenware potter in 1786. He appears
in 1802 in a partnership of Boon & Ridgway and is recorded as a maker of blue-printed
earthenwares. The *Encyclopaedia of British Pottery and Porcelain Marks* states that a
Joseph Boon is recorded as potting between 1784 and 1814.

Booth   Many potters of this name were working during the 1780–1850 period. The
most important firm was Ephraim Booth & Sons of Cliff Bank, Stoke. Hugh Booth, a
Booth, Ephraim & Sons   potter in Stoke, was described in the survey of 1786 as
a manufacturer of china, china-glaze, and Queen's Ware in all its branches. He died
in 1789 and was succeeded by his brother Ephraim, who took his two sons Hugh and
Joseph into partnership, when the firm was styled E. Booth & Sons, and so appears in
the 1802 list. This firm cannot have existed for long after this date, as in 1804 William
Adams took over the Cliff Bank Works, where he started to make his blue-printed
ware. Some authorities list blue-printed among the wares produced by E. Booth &
Sons. The impressed mark E.B. & S. is attributed to them.

Other recorded potters of this name are:

Booth & Co. of Lane End, 1802
Booth, J. & T. of Lane End, 1818
Booth & Sons of Lane End, 1830–5
Booth & Meigh of Lane End, 1828–37
Booth, James of Lane End, fl. 1842.

There was probably some family connection between most of these Lane End potteries.

IRONSTONE is given as a possible mark of Booth & Meigh by the *Encyclopaedia of*
B. & M.

British Pottery and Porcelain Marks.

Bott & Co. of Longton. This impressed mark appears on earthenwares, mainly figures and lustre wares, of the early nineteenth century, and may possibly be found on blue-printed pieces.

There are records of two firms of this name:

Bott, John & Co. of Lane End, Longton, c. 1810
Bott, Thomas & Co. of Lane End, Longton, c. 1811.

Bourne Many potters of this name appear in the history of the Staffordshire Potteries, but little information about them, or their wares, is available with the exception of William Bourne.

Bourne, William of Burslem rented the Bell Works, Burslem, about 1804 and appears in the 1818 directory. He produced large quantities of blue-printed, from which he is said to have made a fortune. At some time after 1818 he entered into partnership with a potter named Cormie, when the style of the firm became Bourne & Cormie.

Bourne & Cormie This partnership must have been of very short duration, as James Cormie (*q.v.*) appears on his own in a directory of 1820, when he had taken the Nile Street Works, Burslem, which J. & R. Riley had vacated when they moved to the Hill Works, Burslem. It is possible that Bourne continued at the Bell Works for a time, but Jewitt states that by 1836 these works had been unoccupied for some time.

It has been surmised that the mark W.B. & C. appearing on blue-printed wares may relate to William Bourne & Co.; alternatively it might be interpreted as W. Bourne & Cormie.

Bourne, Charles of The Foley, Lane Delph, Fenton, appears in the 1818 list of potters and was still operating in 1829. Although appearing on the list of earthenware potters he was chiefly concerned with the manufacture of porcelain. He is said to have succeeded Samuel Spode, who is listed at these works in the 1802 directory.

Bourne, Edward built a factory in Longport about 1790 and continued there until 1811, making earthenwares.

Other recorded potters of this name are:

Bourne, John of Burslem, 1786
Bourne & Co. of Shelton, 1802
Bourne & Malkin of Burslem, 1786
Bourne, Nixon & Co. of Tunstall, 1829.

Bourne & Baker Ralph Bourne and William Baker established a pottery
Bourne, Baker & Bourne in Fenton towards the end of the eighteenth century.
Baker & Co. They appear as Bourne & Baker in the 1802 directory, but at some time later took a further partner, and in 1818 are listed as Bourne, Baker & Bourne. In 1829 they worked two extensive factories in Fenton, and were doing a large home and export trade. In 1843 Ward said that Ralph Bourne was late head of the firm, and that William Baker was now the sole surviving partner. The firm continued as Baker & Co. or W. Baker & Co. until well into the twentieth century. A great deal of blue-printed ware was made, including much of the well-known pattern, common to many factories, of the river, bridge and boat scene. A very large jug of this pattern, 28 inches high, made by this firm in the 1830–40 period, is in the Victoria and Albert Museum and was made as special order for Bailey Neale & Co. of St Paul's Churchyard (pl. 12).

Boyle, Zachariah made china and earthenwares, and is recorded as having a factory in both Hanley and Stoke. He was established in Stoke shortly before 1829, when Shaw gives the style of the firm as Z. Boyle & Son. Jewitt states that Zachariah Boyle died in 1841, but according to most authorities the firm carried on until 1850. The *Encyclopaedia of British Pottery and Porcelain Marks* gives the dates as Hanley 1823–30 and Stoke 1828–50. They made blue-printed earthenwares with the impressed mark BOYLE: alternatively the initials Z.B. or Z.B. & S. appear, sometimes accompanied by the name of the pattern.

A plate in the Victoria and Albert Museum of the well-known Spode 'Blue Italian' pattern has an impressed mark BOYLE (pl. 13). A printed mark 'Boyle & Son, Stoke, Manufacturers' has also been noted on blue-printed earthenwares.

Boyle, John is said to have made earthenwares in Hanley from 1826 until he became a partner of Herbert Minton in the firm Minton & Boyle from 1836 to 1841. In 1843 he joined the firm of Wedgwood, where he remained until he died in 1845.

Breeze, John began potting at some time before 1795, when he is recorded
Breeze, John & Son as being present at a potters' meeting in Burslem. He took
over the Smithfield Works, Tunstall, from Theophilus Smith in 1797, and finally
purchased and renamed them Greenfield in 1801, and appears in the Tunstall list of
the following year. His son Jessie Breeze, born in 1775, joined his father soon after
leaving Repton School, when the firm became John Breeze & Son. At this time the
family worked three potteries, one at Longport, near Burslem, and the Greenfield and
Knowl works, both near Tunstall. The father died in 1821, but had previously given
up the management of the firm to Jessie about 1812. In 1818 the Knowl works were
taken over by Enoch Wood. Jessie continued the Greenfield factory at Tunstall until
his death in 1826. The following year this factory passed to William Adams (1798–
1865) on his marriage to Jane, the eldest daughter of Jessie Breeze. Porcelain formed a
major part of the Breeze output, but blue-printed earthenwares were also made. The
firm had a large export trade with the U.S.A., both before and after the American War
of 1812–15.

Bridgwood of Lane End, Longton. The history of this pottery is very
Bridgwood, S. vague. J. C. Wedgwood* says that: 'Roger Woods is said
Bridgwood, S. & Son to have built in 1756 a factory afterwards known as Sampson
Bridgwoods, by the brook at the Lower Market Place in Longton.' Samuel Bridgwood
appears in the Lane End list of 1802. In 1818 Maria Bridgwood of Market Street and
Kitty Bridgwood & Son of Market Street are both listed in Lane End. Jewitt in 1878
says: 'Sampson Bridgwood & Sons who are extensive manufacturers, first carried on
business in the Market Street Works, and next for many years at a manufactory in
Stafford St., originally occupied by G. Forrester [*q.v.*]. They then removed to their
present works the Anchor Pottery where they produced both china and earthenware.'
Ward in 1843 says that Sampson Bridgwood had three factories in Lane End.

Bridgwood, Goodwin & Orton *see* Goodwin & Orton.

Brooke(s), William The surname is spelt Brooke or Brookes by various authorities.
He was an engraver working first at Tunstall and later at Burslem. He executed some
early engravings for William and Benjamin Adams of Greengates, Tunstall, including
a well-known classical landscape based on a picture by Claude Lorraine (pl. 4). Shaw
states that about 1802 William Brookes made the suggestion to J. Clive of Tunstall of a
new method of decorating borders of blue-printed wares with continuous strip patterns
as then used for borders for wallpaper hangings, a suggestion quickly adopted by most
potters.†
A plate in the Victoria and Albert Museum with a transfer-printed pattern in dark

---

* *Staffordshire Pottery and its History*, p. 111
† Shaw, *op. cit.*, p. 226

blue is labelled 'Printed with a design by William Brooke of Port Vale, Wolstanton, marked with impressed DAVENPORT and anchor 1825–30' (pl. 24). This was his private address when he was working in Burslem. He died in 1838.

Brownfield, William   *see* Robinson, Wood & Brownfield and supplementary list.

Bucknall & Stevenson   In 1770 a Robert Bucknall's signature appears on a list of master potters who formed a ring to keep up prices. In 1786 the same name occurs in the Cobridge directory as a manufacturer of Queen's Ware, blue-painted, enamelled and printed, etc. This name does not appear again until 1808 when Bucknall & Stevenson were in partnership at the Cobridge Works until about 1816, when Bucknall retired. Andrew Stevenson (*q.v.*) continued on his own and became one of the foremost manufacturers of blue-printed. It is most unlikely that the firm of Bucknall & Stevenson (referred to by some authorities as Stevenson & Bucknall) did not make underglaze blue transfer-printed wares. The mark B. & S. below a crown has been recorded and may refer to this firm.

Burrow(s), Joseph   of Fenton is recorded as a maker of printed, painted and lustre wares at The Foley, Fenton, about 1818. On the 1818 list he appears as Joseph Burrow of the Foley Works: perhaps the successor to Arthur Burrow who is listed as a potter supplying goods for sale to the London agents Abbott & Mist (*q.v.*), in their account books at some date between 1801 and 1808.*

Burrows & Co.   Shaw records a firm of this name, among other manufacturers of considerable extent, at Tunstall about 1828.

Burton, Samuel & John   of New Street Pottery, Hanley. The Burtons took over this factory in 1832 from James Keeling (*q.v.*), who had taken a leading part in improving processes in underglaze blue printing. They were still operating when Ward wrote in 1843, but seemingly only remained in business until 1845.

Carey, Thomas & John   of Lane End. This firm seems first to appear in the 1818
Carey & Son   list as Carey & Son. In 1829 Shaw lists Thomas Carey in Lane Delph and T. & J. Carey in Lane End. In 1842, at about the time the firm came to an end, Ward states that T. & J. Carey had one factory at Middle Fenton, lately called Lane Delph, and two at Lane End. They executed many blue-printed patterns (pl. 14). The mark was CAREYS, impressed or printed, sometimes with an anchor. The name of the pattern and type body, such as 'Saxon Stone', was often included in printed marks (fig. 16).

* Bevis Hillier, *The Turners of Lane End*, 1965, p. 64

Challinor, Edward   potted on his own account both in Tunstall and Burslem from about 1819 to 1828 and then became a partner in the firm of Wood & Challinor (*q.v.*), first at Brownhills, and from 1835 at Woodlands, Tunstall, where they are listed by Ward in 1843. Shortly after this date Challinor left the firm and began to operate on his own account again, carrying on in Tunstall until 1867. Marks E.C. or E. CHALLINOR.

Chetham & Woolley   of Commerce Street, Lane End, Longton, were in partner-
Chetham & Son   ship making earthenwares from about 1795 until 1809. In
Chetham & Robinson   November of the latter year, James Chetham having died, the partnership was dissolved and Richard Woolley (*q.v.*) set up on his own and left the old pottery to be carried on by Ann, widow of James Chetham. Ann Chetham took her son into the business as Chetham & Son. Later the firm became Chetham & Robinson, although the two firms appear to have overlapped in dates which, according to the *Encyclopaedia of British Pottery and Porcelain Marks*, were:

Chetham & Son, 1810–34
Chetham & Robinson, 1822–37 (pls. 15 and 16).

Two later firms in Commerce Street, Lane End, Longton, taken from the same source were:

Chetham, Jonathan Lowe   1841–62 (fig. 17)
Chetham, J. R. & F.   1846–69.

Names or initials, according to the partnership, appear on marks of all these firms. Blue-printed earthenware pieces occur with the initials C. & R. Most of these probably refer to Chetham & Robinson but may also have been used by Chesworth & Robinson (*see* supplementary list) (fig. 104).

Child, Smith   of Newfield, Tunstall. These works were erected in 1763 and were carried on by Smith Child until 1790. Specimens of cream-coloured earthenwares with the impressed mark CHILD are recorded, and he may well have introduced blue printing towards the end of his time. His successor J. H. Clive (*q.v.*) took a prominent part in the production of underglaze blue-printed.

Child & Clive   *see* Clive, John Henry.

Clementson, Joseph   of Phoenix Works, Shelton, Hanley. Joseph Clementson occupied these works at some time in the 1830s,* following Elijah Jones who had given up in 1832. Clementson died in 1871, but had previously handed over control of the firm to his four sons, when the firm became Clementson Bros. He used a light blue for his blue-printed wares and exported largely to the U.S.A. He used a printed mark, J.C. or J. CLEMENTSON, sometimes with the word 'Ironstone' or 'Stone China' in a floral scroll. American collecting books record a mark of a spread eagle (possibly a

* *See* Read & Clementson

Phoenix bird) with the word 'Ironstone' above, and 'Sydenham J. Clementson' below, with the explanation that Sydenham was the name of the works which he occupied.

Jewitt states that between 1832 and the time when Joseph Clementson became the sole proprietor about 1839, the firm was Reed & Clementson (*see* Read & Clementson). A fine earthenware blue-printed octagonal dish is illustrated in Geoffrey A. Godden's *Illustrated Encyclopaedia of British Pottery and Porcelain*, 1966, pl. 154, subject 'Nestors Sacrifice', with printed name-mark J. CLEMENTSON.

Clews, James & Ralph rented the Cobridge Works, Cobridge, from William Adams (1748–1831) on 29 September 1817. They were in active operation from early 1818 until 1834, when the firm went bankrupt. In 1836 James Clews went to America and started a pottery at Troy, in Indiana, but soon failed. During their comparatively short tenancy of this factory the Clews brothers produced an enormous quantity of underglaze blue transfer-printed wares, in greater variety perhaps than any other potter. They used a number of different earthenware bodies and their colour varies from a soft light blue to a deep rich blue. They built up a large export trade with America, at first in the well-known dark blue, and later with a large series of American views in different colours, including a light blue.

In addition to a Willow pattern and other oriental designs, many prints of floral, romantic ruins (pl. 17) and pastoral subjects were used. A series of Italianate engravings, almost similar to those of Spode, such as the Tower pattern, were also produced. They are best known for their large selection of English views issued under the headings of 'Select Views' and 'Select Scenery'. These consisted mainly of abbeys, cathedrals, castles and other more general views of towns and cities. These are mainly bordered with one of two floral arrangements, the one with bell- and chrysanthemum-type flowers, and the other with large lily- and camellia-type flowers (pl. 18). Less common on these views is a border of scrolls and foliage.

Many American views have been recorded, some of which were engraved from water colours by W. G. Wall, an Irish artist, who went to America in 1818 for this especial purpose. Sketches by this artist were also used by A. Stevenson, another Cobridge potter, working at the same time as the Clews, some of the pictures being identical. Borders on American views have various arrangements of scrolls and flowers and another with birds, flowers and scrolls. Another border used on the 'Landing of Lafayette' print is mainly of leaves with scattered bunches of small flowers. The most striking American border has, for its main feature, scalloped festoons containing the names of 15 States. These services have central views of the White House and other buildings. It was not until about 1830 that the series called 'Picturesque Views' was issued in light blue and other colours. Their export designs also included a series of French views.

In more original vein are the series of engravings illustrating the three Tours of Doctor Syntax (pls. 19 and 20) and the adventures of Don Quixote, each having the name of the incident printed on the back. These prints and the borders surrounding them have been more fully described earlier in the text. A further set of seven engravings were interpretations of pictures of country life, domestic scenes, painted by Sir David Wilkie. These are named 'Christmas Eve', 'The Errand Boy', 'The Escape of the Mouse', 'Letter of Introduction', 'Playing at Draughts', 'The Rabbit on the Wall' and 'The Valentine' and have a flower border, the passion flower being predominant, and small scrolls. A 'Zoological Garden' series such as 'Bear Cages' and 'Bird Cages' are mainly in colours other than blue, and have a border of twisted scrolls. An unusual piece is illustrated in pl. 21.

While the majority of blue-printed pieces seem to have been marked with the name Clews in some form or other, many pieces have only the name of the pattern, title or view. These appear in various arrangements of scrolls, ribbons or wreaths (figs. 10 and 13). In these cases the border is usually sufficient to identify the piece. The impressed mark is either 'Clews Warranted Staffordshire' with a crown above (fig. 9) or a circular mark with the same words surrounding a crown (fig. 8). The former mark sometimes has the initials G.R. on each side of the crown, which presumably could apply to any date between 1818 and 1830. Alternatively, a printed mark appears with the name Clews printed across a Chinese seal-type mark with the name of the type of body e.g. 'Stone China' underneath (fig. 12). Quite often the printed and impressed marks appear on the same piece. An unusual mark (fig. 11) on blue-printed ware recorded by Chaffers presumably applies to the year 1820 or 1830.

Clive, John Henry of Newfield, Tunstall, took over in 1802 the factory which had been occupied earlier by Smith Child (*q.v.*) and is reputed to have been one of the earliest and most successful pioneers in the introduction of ornamental engravings into the blue-printed trade. William Brooke(s), an engraver, living at that time at Tunstall, probably produced the engravings for Clive. According to Shaw it was this potter who first adopted the suggestion made by Brooke(s), about 1802, of using continuous strips of repeat patterns for border designs for plates and dishes, as then used for borders for wallpaper hangings. His mark was CLIVE impressed. After 1811 the firm was Child & Clive and is so listed in 1818. This firm probably lasted until 1828, when the **Child & Clive** factory was taken over by Joseph Heath & Co.

Copeland & Garrett⎫
　　　　　　　　　　⎬ *see* Spode.
Copeland, W. T.⎭

Cork & Condliffe of Queen Street, Burslem, are listed by Ward in 1842 and may have been the predecessors of Cork & Edge.

Cork & Edge of Newport Pottery, Burslem, made earthenwares from 1846–60, and were succeeded by Cork, Edge & Malkin. Various printed marks occur on blue-printed with the initials C. & E. and C.E. & M. (fig. 18).

Cormie, James previously a partner in Bourne & Cormie (*q.v.*), Burslem, appears in a directory of 1820 as the proprietor of the Nile Street Works, Burslem, previously occupied by J. & R. Riley. In 1829 Shaw lists J. Cormie as occupying one of the six largest potteries in Burslem, with an added note that he did a large export trade with Europe and America. He is not mentioned by Ward in 1842.

Cutts, James was a skilful engraver working in Shelton from about 1834 to 1870. He is said to have engraved some patterns for Wedgwood's. His signature is occasionally found on printed patterns.

Cyples A family of potters of this name in Lane End, Longton, who covered practically the whole period from 1780–1850. Joseph Cyples of Market Street, Longton, who made black basalt wares and pottery in general, appears in the 1786 list. He is replaced in the 1802 list by Mary Cyples, probably his widow, who in turn, in the 1818 list, was succeeded by Lydia Cyples. The firm subsequently became R. & W. Cyples, Cyples, Barlow & Cyples and in 1849 Thomas Barlow.

The dates given by the *Encyclopaedia of British Pottery and Porcelain Marks* are:

Joseph Cyples, c. 1784–95
Mary Cyples, c. 1795–1812
Jesse Cyples, c. 1805–11
Lydia Cyples, c. 1812–34
R. & W. Cyples, c. 1834–40
Cyples, Barlow & Cyples, c. 1841–48.

Cyples & Barker of Market Street, Longton, 1846–7.

Dale, John of Burslem is recorded as potting in the early nineteenth century. An impressed mark I. DALE or J. DALE BURSLEM appears on earthenware figures. One writer makes reference to Willow pattern plates and dishes with this mark, but this appears to be doubtful.

Daniel Many potters of this name are recorded, but little is known of most of them, or their wares.

Daniel, Henry & Richard of Shelton and Stoke made good-quality porcelain and
Daniel, Richard earthenwares. According to Shaw the Stoke factory was confined wholly to china and Shelton to earthenwares. Henry Daniel, who had been employed at the Spode factory, set up with his son Richard as a master potter

about 1820. Henry is said to have died in 1841, although Ward still lists the firm as H. & R. Daniel in 1843 without any mention of the firm at Shelton. In 1829 Shaw lists H. & R. Daniel at Stoke making china only and at Shelton he lists Henry Daniel & Sons. Richard Daniel gave up the Shelton works on his father's death, so that any blue-printed wares made by this firm would have been produced at Shelton between 1820–41 and could be marked H. & R. Daniel or H. Daniel & Sons. Richard Daniel continued the Stoke works until about 1854.

Other recorded potters of this name are:

Daniel, John   listed in 1786 at Burslem, mainly known as a maker and decorator of cream-coloured wares.
Daniel, Thomas   listed in 1786 at Burslem.
Daniel, Timothy   listed in 1786 at Burslem.
Daniel, Walter   listed in 1786 and 1802 in Burslem. Jewitt states that he established the Newport Pottery, Burslem, which was taken over, and added to his other factories, by John Davenport about 1810.
Daniel, S.   of Stoke. This signature is recorded underneath designs on black-printed wares. He was probably an engraver rather than a manufacturer, and may have been a member of a decorating establishment c. 1805–15.

Davenport   John Davenport, born in 1765, is said to have begun potting in 1785, first as a workman, and later as a partner with Thomas Wolfe of Stoke. He acquired his own pottery at Longport for the manufacture of earthenwares in 1794. In 1830 he retired, and his two sons Henry and William carried on the firm until 1835, when Henry died. The style of the firm then became William Davenport & Co. William died in 1869, and his two sons took over the direction of the business, which remained in the family until 1887.

At the beginning, earthenwares only were made, of which blue-printed formed a large part. Porcelain was not manufactured until about 1815. During the whole existence of the firm underglaze blue transfer-printed earthenwares were made in very large quantities. Many different bodies were used, including a stone china. The blue varies from a light to a medium colour.* Willow patterns were made extensively, and unlike most of the other potters, *chinoiseries* of different designs remained one of the chief motifs of their printed patterns over the whole period (pl. 22). These are seen on every conceivable type of domestic wares. Baskets with openwork sides, and plates and dishes with pierced and wicker pattern borders, were made in quantity. Other designs of floral patterns, romantic ruins and pastoral scenes (pl. 23) were used. No named English scenic views appear to have been made, nor did the firm cater for the American market in this type of ware, although a view of the city of Montreal is recorded in one American book on pottery.

* A marked plate in the Victoria and Albert Museum in an unusually dark blue for this factory is printed with a design by William Brooke(s) (pl. 24)

It is probable that many of the earliest pieces were not marked, but judging from the number of nineteenth-century pieces which may still be found it must have been rare for a piece made after 1800 not to have been marked. The earliest mark was the name 'Davenport', impressed in lower-case letters, with or without an anchor. After about 1805, the name more often appears in upper-case letters. Occasionally the anchor appears alone. The word 'Longport' is sometimes substituted for Davenport.

Deakin & Bailey   The Hanley Museum and Art Gallery have several well-executed blue-printed parts of dinner services with a printed mark with the title CRUSADERS in a foliated cartouche and the name Deakin & Bailey beneath (fig. 19). These appear to be of the 1830–40 period. The *Encyclopaedia of British Pottery and Porcelain Marks* gives this firm as of Lane End, c. 1828–30.

Deakin & Son   of Lane End had two potteries according to Ward in his list of about 1842. The *Encyclopaedia of British Pottery and Porcelain Marks* gives the dates as 1833–41 with the note that at later dates the style was James Deakin & Co. and/or James Deakin & Son.

Dillon   A pottery in the name of Frank & N. Dillon was listed at Cobridge in 1818 and was probably established a year or two before that date. By 1829 the style of the firm was N. Dillon and in 1834 became Francis Dillon and was still operating in the same name, or as Francis Dillon & Co., in 1843. They are recorded as making blue-printed earthenwares, including some scriptural designs. The mark would be DILLON or the relevant initials, sometimes with the name of the pattern.

Dimmock & Co.   In 1818 a firm called Hackwood, Dimmock & Co. (*q.v.*) was listed at Hanley. This Hackwood was the son of William Hackwood, Wedgwood's modeller, and is said to have entered into partnership with John Dimmock for the manufacture of earthenwares about 1816. By 1827 Hackwood's name had disappeared* and in 1829 Shaw lists Dimmock & Co. as the largest pottery in Hanley. This appears to be the same firm that became Thomas Dimmock & Co., which Ward states had three factories in Hanley and Shelton in 1843. He may have been referring to the two firms listed in the *Encyclopaedia of British Pottery and Porcelain Marks*, namely:

Thomas Dimmock (Junr.) & Co., Albion Street (c. 1829–59), Tontine Street (c. 1830–50), Shelton (also at Hanley).
Dimmock & Smith, Tontine Street, Hanley, 1826–33 and 1842–59.

The initial D is recorded as appearing on several different printed marks in which the name of the pattern was sometimes included.

* The reference to this firm in the *Belle Vue Papers* of 1823 is to T. Dimmock alone

Donovan, James This name occasionally appears impressed in large capital letters on Staffordshire blue-printed earthenwares (pl. 49). M. S. D. Westropp in *Irish Pottery and Porcelain*, published in 1935, states that the name of this Dublin glass and china merchant and decorator appears in Dublin Directories from about 1770 until 1829. From 1818 the entry is in the name of the son, James Donovan Junior. The name has been recorded, painted, stencilled and impressed on pottery and porcelain of various kinds. The impressed name has been noted on pieces of blue-printed earthenware, which also bear the impressed name 'ROGERS'.

Dudson, James of Hanley. Jewitt states that he took over the Hope Street Works, Hanley, in 1835 and was still carrying on at the time he wrote in 1878. He specialised in figures and ornamental stone and jasper wares. Ward in 1843 makes no mention of this firm but lists only Richard Dudson of Hanley, described by Ward as a china
Dudson, Richard manufacturer who had taken over a factory formerly occupied by William Rivers & Co. (*q.v.*) who made earthenwares from about 1818–22.

The *Encyclopaedia of British Pottery and Porcelain Marks* suggests that the initials R.D. on earthenwares may apply to Richard Dudson of Hanley c. 1838–44, or alternatively to Richard Daniel (*q.v.*).

Eastwood *see* Baddeley, William.

Edge, Daniel of Burslem. The only potter of this name mentioned by Ward in 1842 is Daniel Edge of Waterloo Road, Burslem, who was the same potter who had been in partnership with Samuel Grocott as Edge & Grocott, earthenware figure makers, at Tunstall in the early 1830s. It was presumably soon after this that he started on his own at Burslem, but gave up shortly after the time at which Ward was writing.

Other partnerships recorded in the *Encyclopaedia of British Pottery and Porcelain Marks* are:
Edge, William & Samuel of Market Street, Lane Delph, 1841–8
Edge, Barker & Co. of Fenton and Lane End, 1835–6
Edge, Barker & Barker of Fenton, 1836–40.

Various marks printed in blue with the name of the pattern, usually with an urn on the left hand side, and the initials E.B. & CO. appearing on plates with an underglaze blue-printed pattern probably refer to Edge, Barker & Co. (fig. 20).

Edwards, James of Burslem started as a workman with J. & G. Rogers of Longport, and later became manager to E. & G. Phillips of the same town, both firms being noted makers of blue-printed. Jewitt states that Edwards took the Kilncroft Works, Burslem in 1825 but this appears to be too early. He was first a partner in Maddock & Edwards (*q.v.*) in Burslem until about 1839, when he occupied the Kilncroft Works with his brother Thomas as a partner.

Edwards, James & Thomas   of Kilncroft Works, Burslem, are listed by Ward in 1843. This partnership ended at this time and James purchased on his own account the Dale Hall Pottery previously worked by J. Rogers & Son. The style of the firm became James Edwards, until he took his son Richard into partnership in 1851 as

Edwards, James   James Edwards & Son. This firm continued for another

Edwards, James & Son   30 years under the same name, although the father died in 1867. Blue-printed wares were made during these various partnerships, with printed or impressed marks, EDWARDS, J. & T.E. or the names and initials in full. A large export trade was carried on with America, mainly transfer-printed wares in the later colours, including a series called 'Boston Mails' showing interior views of cabins on a steamboat. These were made during the partnership J. & T. Edwards. The mark was a sailing ship with BOSTON MAILS above and EDWARDS below.

Elkin(s) & Co.   This firm began to operate about 1820 and continued under a variety of trading names until 1853. They made china and earthenwares and were extensive manufacturers of 'Willow' and 'Broseley' patterns and other blue-printed services. In 1829 Shaw lists the firm at The Foley, Fenton, as Elkin, Knight & Bridgwood with the comment that this pottery 'is a new and very complete establishment'. In 1843 Ward mentions them as Knight, Elkin & Bridgwood and Jewitt states that subsequently, on the retirement of Elkin, the works were carried on by John King Knight alone until 1853. He was then joined in partnership by Henry Wileman as Knight & Wileman until 1856, when the latter carried on alone until his death in 1864.

   During their existence of some 30 years there was an extraordinarily complicated variation of different partnerships. A full list compiled from the rate records as given by the *Encyclopaedia of British Pottery and Porcelain Marks* is as follows:

Elkins & Co.   of Lane End, c. 1822–30 (this is possibly the beginning of the firm when the partners were Elkin, Knight & Elkin)

Elkin Knight & Co.   of the Foley Potteries, Fenton, 1822–6

Elkin, Knight & Bridgwood   of the Foley Potteries, Fenton, c. 1827–40—also known as Knight, Elkin & Co. or Knight, Elkin & Bridgwood

Knight Elkin & Co.   of the Foley Potteries, Fenton, 1826–40—also trading as Knight & Elkin

Knight, Elkin & Knight   of King Street, Fenton, 1841–4—also trading as Knight, Elkin & Co.

Knight, John King   of the Foley Potteries, Fenton, 1846–53.

The marks may be the initials of any of the above partnerships (fig. 21). The initials K.E.B. have been noted on blue-printed earthenwares and appear to be of the right date to relate to Knight, Elkin & Bridgwood. A blue-printed piece is illustrated which has a printed mark ELKINS & CO. with the pre-1837 Royal Arms and the title 'Irish Scenery' (pl. 25) (fig. 103). This would appear to refer to Elkin, Knight & Elkin.

Fletcher, Thomas & Co. Thomas Fletcher, an engraver, black printer and enameller, established his decorating establishment in Shelton shortly before 1786 and continued until about 1810. A number of signed pieces with overglaze black prints are recorded. They are of various subjects, including a fine print of a cricket match at Lords between the Earls of Winchelsea and Darnley for 1,000 guineas, taken from an engraving by Cook published in the *Sporting Magazine* for June 1793. Similar prints of cricket matches appear on blue-printed earthenwares. Thomas Fletcher may well have produced engravings for underglaze as well as overglaze printing.

Folch, Stephen of Stoke. Chaffers records a plate with coloured transfer printing with the mark FOLCH'S GENUINE STONE CHINA of the 1820–30 period. A large blue-printed version of the pre-1837 Royal Arms sometimes forms part of the mark.

Forester, Thomas of Lane Delph appears in the 1802 list which becomes George
Forrester, George Forrester in 1818 in Market Place, Lane End. Chaffers writes that George Forrester had a manufactory in Lane End in the first quarter of the nineteenth century and was doing good business in 1823 and 1829. Shaw, writing of the same pottery in the Market Place, says: 'Mr. G. Forrester's Manufactory, which appears to have been the first in which a regular plan for the arrangement of the separate places for the distinct processes was adopted. It is not large, but very convenient.'

Furnival, J. & T. The Furnivals followed Reuben Johnson at Miles Bank,
Furnival, T. & Co. Hanley (*q.v.*) about 1840, when the firm was probably Jacob & Thomas Furnival. Ward in 1843 lists the firm as Thomas Furnival (Junr.) & Co. In 1846 the firm became Furnival & Clark until 1851. The mark T.F. & CO. appears on printed wares.

Furnival, Jacob & Co. of Cobridge began making earthenwares about 1845. Blue-printed wares with the initials J.F. & CO. were exported to America.

Gallimore, Robert rented the St James Works, Longton, in 1831, although one authority states that previous to this the firm was A. & R. Gallimore. In 1840 Gallimore took George Shubotham (quoted by various writers as Shufflebotham, Shutbotham and Shubotham) when the firm was styled Gallimore & Shubotham. In 1842 Gallimore retired and was replaced by William Webberley as Shubotham & Webberley. In 1847 Shubotham died and the works were carried on by Webberley alone. Writing about 1842, Ward not only quotes Gallimore & Shufflebotham in Lane End, but shows that R. Gallimore had also taken a factory previously occupied by Joseph Myatt in The Foley, Fenton. The Longton firm specialised in lustre wares, but made general earthenwares as well, and, according to Jewitt, china only, after 1844.

Garner, Robert   born in 1733, learnt his trade with Thomas Whieldon, along with Josiah Spode and others, who later became celebrated master potters. Later Garner began potting at Foley, Fenton, in partnership with others, but subsequently erected his own factory in Lane End, where he is listed in 1786. He died in 1789 and was succeeded by his son, also Robert, who had been born in 1766. The latter is listed at 'Lane End, now called Longton' making general earthenwares in 1802 and 1818. He is said to have continued until about 1821, although Shaw writes as if he was still active in 1829.

Garner, Joseph   is listed as a potter in Lane End in 1786.

Gerrard   Shaw,* speaking of the early nineteenth century says: 'Several other manufacturers now commenced manufacturing Blue Printed Pottery. The late Mr. Jas Gerrard with Mr. Jas Keeling, of New Street, Hanley, introduced some improvements in the processes.' Shaw is speaking of James Keeling of Hanley (*q.v.*) who was potting from c. 1796–1830. There is no record of any master potter James Gerrard at this time. He may have been an employee or engraver working with Keeling or an unrecorded predecessor of one of the firms recorded in the *Encyclopaedia of British Pottery and Porcelain Marks*, namely:

Gerrard, John   of Hanley, c. 1824–36
Gerrard, John   of Hanley, c. 1846–53.

Ginder, Samuel & Co.   of Victoria Works, Lane Delph, Fenton, made many types of earthenware from 1811 and is still listed by Ward as Ginder & Co. in 1843, about which time the pottery closed. Shaw refers to S. Ginders of Lane Delph who occupied the manufactory erected by the younger Astbury (*q.v.*).

Glass, John   of Market Street, Hanley, earthenware potter, is listed in Hanley in 1786 and in 1802. In 1818 and 1821 the firm appears as John Glass & Sons. The firm continued until the end of the 1830s and in 1840 the pottery was taken over by Samuel Keeling & Co. The *Encyclopaedia of British Pottery and Porcelain Marks* gives the three phases of the firm as:

> John Glass, c. 1784–1812
> John Glass & Sons, c. 1818–22
> John Glass, c. 1822–38.

Impressed mark: GLASS HANLEY

Godwin   Thomas and Benjamin Godwin, probably brothers, began potting in Cobridge at some time before 1786, in which year they are listed in the directory as

* Shaw, *op. cit.*, p. 214

makers of Queen's Ware and china glazed blue. At a later date the family founded potteries in Burslem. The various partnerships, judging from surviving records, were approximately as follows:

Cobridge

Godwin, Thomas & Benjamin were making cream-coloured and pearl wares at Cobridge by 1786. Either they or their sons had split up by 1802, when the directory shows two separate factories, one occupied by T. Godwin and the other by B. Godwin. This dissolution of partnership had apparently happened before 1795 when they are shown as two separate entries at a meeting of potters in Burslem on 30 April in that year. About 1809 these two appear to have joined up again and transferred their business to Burslem (*see* next entry). From about the same date the Cobridge pottery appears as B. & S. Godwin. The same partnership appears in the 1818 directory and remained so until some time before 1829 when the firm is listed by Shaw in the sole name of S. Godwin. About 1834 a further division took place, one pottery being conducted by Benjamin Endon Godwin, and the other by John and Robert Godwin. In 1843 Ward lists these two firms and another in the names of John Mayer Godwin and James Godwin.* John and Robert Godwin continued until 1864, but Benjamin E. Godwin ceased potting about the time that Ward was writing. The initials of the various partnerships may appear as marks. B.G. appears on several printed marks of the flowery and foliated cartouche type which are attributed to, and are typical of the period of, Benjamin E. Godwin. J. & R.G. appears on printed marks of different design on several blue-printed patterns.

Burslem

Godwin, Thomas & Benjamin began potting at the New Basin pottery in Burslem about 1809, and later at a pottery in Burslem Wharf. This partnership lasted until 1834, when Benjamin disappears and the business is in the sole name of T. Godwin. Ward lists the pottery as Thomas Godwin of Burslem Wharf in 1843, and it is still so listed in a directory of 1851.

Names or initials of both styles are recorded on various printed marks, sometimes with the addition of New Wharf. Thomas Godwin is the only potter of all the Godwin family on record as having made transfer-printed wares with American scenic views. These were carried out in various colours including a light blue. Sometimes the type of body used, such as Stone China or Opaque China, is included in the mark. Occasionally the mark was a small printed scene of buildings and trees with a reserved space for the name of the pattern and the initials T.G. (fig. 22). This mark appears on a small series of 'William Penn's treaty with the Indians', the title being on a scroll below the engraving: this series is usually in the later colours. A misleading mark, which puzzled early collectors, was T. GODWIN WHARF, Burslem being omitted.

Plates and dishes are sometimes eight-sided or with scalloped rims. Favourite

---

* *See* supplementary list

borders were geometric patterns, or an arrangement of morning glory- and nasturtium-type flowers.

The partnership between Thomas and Benjamin Godwin is shown on printed marks, with the name of the scene or pattern, either as T. & B.G. or T.B.G. (pl. 26) (fig. 23).

Goodfellow, Thomas   of Tunstall appears to have been the same potter in the partnership of Bathwell and Goodfellow (*q.v.*) at the Upper House Works, Burslem, and another pottery in Tunstall from about 1818–22. Thomas Goodfellow took over the Phoenix Works, Tunstall, at some time after this date and is listed by Shaw about 1828. He continued the works until 1860, when they were pulled down. The mark was T. GOODFELLOW on various printed designs, sometimes with the name of the pattern added.

Goodfellow & Bathwell   *see* Bathwell & Goodfellow.

Goodwin & Co.   of Lane End. According to Chaffers this firm existed at some
Goodwin & Orton   time in the first quarter of the nineteenth century. As it is not listed in the 1818 directory it was presumably founded shortly after this date. Shaw shows the firm as Bridgwood, Goodwin & Orton in 1829, probably in error for Goodwin, Bridgwood & Orton. Thereafter there were many rapid changes of partnership which, as listed in the *Encyclopaedia of British Pottery and Porcelain Marks*, were:

Goodwin, Bridgwood & Orton   1827–9
Goodwin, Bridgwood & Harris   1829–31
Goodwins & Harris   c. 1831–8
Goodwin & Ellis   c. 1839–40—subsequently John Goodwin (*see* below).

The initials of these firms appear on various printed marks. Goodwins & Harris appears in full, sometimes with a lion crest. A printed lion mark without initials may apply to this firm. Chaffers illustrates an ornate printed mark, headed BYRON GALLERY, with a quotation, and the initials G.H. & G. This appears on a blue-printed dish and is shown, without comment, under the heading of Goodwin. Although it does not appear to fit any of the initials of the above firms, or, for that matter, any other known firm, it would be the correct period and might signify Goodwin, Harris & Goodwin which was normally abbreviated to Goodwins & Harris.

Goodwin, John   In 1841 Ward lists John Goodwin as the sole survivor and he appears to have continued until about 1850. Chaffers describes how a Mr Goodwin of Lane End built a factory at Seacombe on the opposite side of the Mersey from Liverpool in 1851, most of the workmen coming from Staffordshire. The first oven was fired in June 1852, and the output consisted mainly of blue and colour-printed ware.

Green, Thomas Jewitt states that the Churchyard Works, Burslem, were sold to Thomas Green in 1795. He appears in the 1802 directory of Burslem potters and remained in these works until he went bankrupt in 1811. The same authority says that Thomas Green, son of Thomas Green of the Churchyard Works, Burslem, joined a Mr Hassall about 1833–4 at the Minerva Works, Fenton. Soon afterwards Hassall **Green & Richards** retired and the firm became Green & Richards and continued until 1847, when Richards retired, and the firm became Thomas Green alone, until his death in 1859. Ward lists Green & Richards in 1843 as china manufacturers. In fact, they made earthenwares as well, including many toy sets, although china was for much of the time their chief product. The mark from 1847 onwards was T. GREEN FENTON POTTERIES, or a Staffordshire knot, T. G. & FENTON being within the loops, and a crown above.

Griffiths, Thomas & Co. of Lane End, Longton. The early history of this **Griffiths, Beardmore & Birks** firm is obscure. One authority states that a **Beardmore & Birks** Thomas Beardmore established the Heathcote Road Pottery, Longton, in the early part of the nineteenth century. The only firm listed is Beardmore & Carr of Lane End in 1818. Ward lists Beardmore & Birks of Lane End, Longton, in 1841. Jewitt says that Beardmore & Birks occupied St Gregory's Pottery, High Street, Longton, originally built by George Barnes in 1794, before it was taken over by George Townsend. The latter occupied the factory about 1850. The *Encyclopaedia of British Pottery and Porcelain Marks* gives Griffiths, Beardmore & Birks of Flint Street, Lane End, 1830, formerly Thomas Griffiths & Co., subsequently Beardmore & Birks. The dates of Beardmore & Birks appear, thus, to be c. 1831–1850.

A Willow pattern dish in the Godden collection bears the initials G.B. & B., the preVictorian Royal Arms and the words 'Staffordshire Ironstone China', which may well apply to the Griffiths, Beardmore & Birks partnership. The same Royal Arms appear with the initials B.B. and probably were used by their successors Beardmore & Birks.

Hackwood of Eastwood, Hanley. This firm, which appears in **Hackwood & Co.** several different styles, made earthenwares at **W. Hackwood & Co.** Eastwood, Hanley, from 1807–27. In 1818 the only **Hackwood, Dimmock & Co.** firm listed is Hackwood, Dimmock & Co, and is almost certainly the same firm. Dimmock left the firm about 1827 to start his own pottery as Dimmock & Co. (*q.v.*) when the firm was registered in the sole name of William Hackwood, and is so listed by Shaw in 1829, and again by Ward in 1843, at which time the firm appears to have come to an end. Marks, either printed or impressed may take any of the above forms, or simply H. or H. & CO. (pl. 27).

Hackwood, William & Thomas of New Hall Pottery, Shelton. The manufacture **Hackwood, William & Son** of porcelain having ceased at the New Hall **Hackwood, Thomas** Pottery, Shelton, it was reopened in 1831 by

William Ratcliffe (*q.v.*) who, for some not very obvious reason, marked some of his white and printed earthenwares with the letter R above the word HACKWOOD printed or impressed (fig. 43). In 1842 the factory passed into the hands of the Hackwoods, and first became William & Thomas Hackwood, then William Hackwood & Son until 1849, when William died and the pottery was continued by Thomas Hackwood until 1856. The firm then became Cockson & Harding who marked their wares C. & H. LATE HACKWOOD. Printed marks occur with the initials W.H. & S.

Hackwood & Keeling of Hanley, a short-lived firm who worked in 1835–6 and marked their wares with the initials H. & K. on various printed marks, often with the name of the pattern included.

Hales & Adams of Cobridge. At some time after his marriage in 1769 William Adams (1748–1831) of Brickhouse, Burslem and Cobridge, entered into a partnership with his step-father John Hales (1736–91). The firm is listed at Cobridge in 1786, and presumably came to an end in 1791, when Hales died. William Adams had produced blue-printed wares at his own main pottery in Cobridge shortly after 1780, so Hales & Adams may well have done the same.

Hall, John & Ralph were partners at the Sytch Pottery, Burslem, from very shortly after 1802 until 1822, and also for some years until the same date at the Swan Bank Works, Tunstall, where they made general earthenwares, including blue-printed. In 1822 they separated, John staying at the Sytch Pottery and Ralph taking over the Swan Bank Works.

Hall, John after dissolving partnership with Ralph Hall in 1822, continued to operate the Sytch Pottery, Burslem, together with his sons. Shaw in 1829 lists them **Hall, John & Sons** as one of the six largest potteries in Burslem who were exporting to both Europe and America. In spite of this they went bankrupt in 1832, and were succeeded by Barker, Sutton & Till (*q.v.*). They made a series of foreign views named 'Oriental', 'Italian' and 'Indian' scenery, some taken from Buckingham's *Travels in Mesopotamia* published in 1828. The mark may be I. HALL or I. HALL & SONS, usually with the name of the pattern in decorative scrolls (fig. 24).

Hall, Ralph When the partnership with John Hall was dissolved in 1822,
Hall, R. & Son Ralph carried on at the Swan Bank Works, Tunstall. At some
Hall, R. & Co. time in the mid-1830s the firm became R. Hall & Son. R. Hall died in 1838, and about 1840 the firm became R. Hall & Co. It is possibly to this latter style that Ward refers, in his 1843 list of Tunstall potters, as Hall & Holland. The firm continued until 1849 and was subsequently taken over as one of the Podmore, Walker & Co. group of factories (*q.v.*). Ralph Hall carried on a large export trade with America, mainly with his English views, and later with some American subject prints. The

English pictures were issued under two headings, 'Select Views' with a border of fruit and flowers with a lace edge, and 'Picturesque Scenery', with a border of large flowers. These were all in dark blue with the name of the scene printed on the reverse in a decorative scroll (fig. 26). Many different printed and impressed marks were used, incorporating the name or initials of any of the above titles of the firm, usually accompanied with the name of the individual pattern. A printed mark with the name R. HALL appears on a series called 'Italian Buildings' in a decorative cartouche (pl. 28) (fig. 25).

Hamilton, Robert of Stoke had previously been in partnership with his father-in-law Thomas Wolfe (*q.v.*), an early manufacturer of blue-printed earthenwares. Hamilton began potting on his own account in 1811, and continued until 1826.

Marks, impressed or printed: $\dfrac{\text{HAMILTON}}{\text{STOKE}}$

Harding & Cockson of Cobridge. Wingfield Harding and Charles Cockson established an earthenware pottery at Cobridge in 1834. The latter died in 1856 and the firm came to an end a few years later.

The name of the firm in full, or the initials H. & C., appear on the mark, often with COBRIDGE added.

Harley, Thomas of Lane End began to make general earthenwares, including transfer-printed wares, about 1802. The mark was HARLEY or T. HARLEY printed or impressed, sometimes with LANE END added. Some printed wares have the name T. HARLEY as part of the decoration. After a few years Harley took a partner and the **Harley & Seckerson** firm became Harley & Seckerson, and is so listed in the directory of 1818. The *Encyclopaedia of British Pottery and Porcelain Marks* states that prior to 1802 Thomas Harley was in partnership with J. G. & W. Weston. The name of George Weston* of Lane End appears in both the 1802 and 1818 lists as a master potter.

Harrison, George
Harrison, George & Co.
Harrison & Hyatt of Lane Delph, Fenton, was an earthenware manufacturer operating in the last decade of the eighteenth century. Jewitt mentions an invoice of 20 August 1793 for parts of dinner services. Both blue-painted and blue-printed wares are recorded with the name G. Harrison impressed in lower-case letters. By 1795 the firm had become George Harrison & Co. of Lower Lane, Fenton, and by 1802, at the same address, and presumably still the same firm, Harrison & Hyatt.

Harrison, John was potting at Cliffgate Bank, Stoke, in 1802.

Harvey, Charles of Lane End, Longton. Jewitt states that the Stafford Street Works, Longton, were built in 1799 by John & Charles Harvey. In the 1802 directory

* *See* supplementary list

the name of Charles Harvey appears alone, as owning two factories in Lane End. By 1818
Harvey, Charles & Sons the firm is listed as Charles Harvey & Sons of Great
Charles Street, Lane End. According to Shaw, Charles Harvey gave up potting soon
after this to become a banker at Longton.

Harvey, C. & W. K. The Stafford Street Works had been taken over by Hulme &
Hawley from Charles Harvey, but were retaken by Charles & W. K. Harvey, sons of
the original Charles Harvey, in 1835, and by 1841 Ward states that they had three
factories in Longton. They continued until 1853, and were succeeded by Holland &
Green. Early marks HARVEY impressed, later C. & W.K.H. printed (pl. 29).

Heath a confusing number of potters of this name operated in the Staffordshire
Potteries during the eighteenth and nineteenth centuries. These are listed under the
various towns.

Burslem
Heath, John of Sytch Pottery, Burslem, appears in the 1818 directory. The
Encyclopaedia of British Pottery and Porcelain Marks gives the dates as 1809–23, and
the mark as HEATH impressed.

Heath, Lewis is said to have started potting at the Hadderidge Manufactory,
Burslem before 1780 and appears in the 1802 directory and probably continued until
1812 when he was followed by his son, Thomas.

Heath, Thomas of Hadderidge, Burslem, is possibly the same T. Heath mentioned by Jewitt as being the managing man of Lakin & Poole, of Hadderidge, Burslem
about 1793. He began potting on his own account. presumably following directly
after his father, Lewis Heath, in 1812. He is mentioned by Shaw in 1829 as owning one
of the largest potteries in Burslem and exporting wares to both Europe and America.
He died in 1839. His mark was T. HEATH with or without BURSLEM. A curious mark on
a blue-printed dish is illustrated by Chaffers showing an elaborate printed mark with
'Sporting Subjects' above and T. HEATH BURSLEM below, superimposed over the impressed mark DAVENPORT. This decoration must have been by some special arrangement between Heath and Davenport whose pottery was in the adjoining hamlet of
Longport.

Heath, Nathan & John of Burslem appear in the 1802 directory.

Heath & Son of Burslem, stated by Jewitt to have worked in the late eighteenth,
and early nineteenth centuries: nothing further of their wares appears to be recorded.
HEATH & SON as an impressed mark is given by most authorities.

Tunstall
Heath, Joseph & Co. of Newfield Pottery, Tunstall, took over the factory from
Child & Clive in 1828 and were still in occupation in 1842 according to Ward's list of

Tunstall potters, when the firm appears to have come to an end. They made large quantities of blue-printed wares, including Willow pattern and flow-blue designs. They exported largely to America including some American views, most of which were in the later colours, other than blue. Various printed marks bear the name J. HEATH & CO. or the initials J.H. & CO. or I.H. & CO.

Heath, Joseph   of Tunstall, probably of the same family as the above firm, operated for a few years from 1845.

Shelton, Hanley

Heath, J.   of Hanley is probably the Joshua Heath who signed a price agreement ring of Staffordshire potters in 1770 and continued to make earthenwares until about 1800. He made cream-coloured wares, blue-painted wares and was one of the early makers of blue-printed, using the usual *chinoiserie*-type patterns. One of his patterns was the 'Buffalo' design (pl. 31), also used by Spode, and probably designed by Minton.

He used the impressed marks I.H. or HEATH. An interesting sauce-boat in the Victoria and Albert Museum with the Buffalo pattern has the mark I.H. in raised moulded letters (pl. 32).

Heath & Bagnall   of Shelton appear in the 1786 directory.

Heath & Shorthose   of Hanley appear in the 1802 directory, but *see* Shorthose & Heath.

Heathcote, Charles & Co.   of Lane End were not established in time to be included in the 1818 directory, but began potting at about that time and continued until 1824. They made good quality blue-printed wares. At some time they are said to have bought some copper plates from Turner of Lane End, and a marked Heathcote plate in the Hanley Museum has identical underglaze printing with a marked Turner plate in the same Museum.* Several printed marks were used with the name C. HEATHCOTE & CO., often with the Prince of Wales' feather crest (figs. 28 and 29). The name of the pattern e.g. CAMBRIA is often included. The impressed name HEATHCOTE & CO. is also found on blue-printed wares (pl. 30).

Henshall & Co.   of Longport, Burslem. The history of this firm
Henshall, Williamson & Clowes   is fragmentary. Jewitt mentions a factory built
Henshall, Williamson & Co.   in Longport shortly after 1773 by Robert Williamson 'who in 1775 married Anne (née Henshall) widow of James Brindley, the engineer'.† A firm by the name of Henshall, Williamson & Clowes appear on a list of Burslem, Tunstall and Cobridge potters at a meeting on 30 April 1795. The *Encyclopaedia of British Pottery and Porcelain Marks* gives the dates of this partnership as

* B. Hillier, *op. cit.*, p. 76
† Jewitt, *op. cit.*, vol. 2, p. 283

c. 1790–5. In 1802 two firms appear in the Longport directory: Henshall, Williamson & Co. and Williamson & Henshall. In 1818 Henshall & Williamson only are quoted, and they also appear on a list of 1823 of Staffordshire potters supplied with potters' materials by the Belle Vue Pottery, Hull. It would appear that the name of Henshall disappeared from the partnership before 1828, as Shaw mentions only 'Messrs Williamson of Longport who had an extensive manufactory' in 1829. Jewitt states that the factory built by Robert Williamson was bought by Henry Davenport just previous to his death in 1835, to add to his other factories and this appears to be borne out by the fact that Ward makes no mention of the factory in 1843. There may be a connection between the original firm and the one Jewitt writes about, when, speaking about Fenton and district, he says: 'Hugh Williamson was a potter in the latter part of last century, and principally made the ordinary blue-printed ware. A plate or tray with blue flowers and border is in the Mayer collection, and is labelled as "Made at Hugh Williamson's". It was transferred by Mrs. Hancock, seventy eight years of age, when she was an apprentice.'[*] Chaffers records a plate in the Sheldon collection with the mark HENSHALL & CO. A plate in the Victoria and Albert Museum with a well-printed design in underglaze blue labelled c. 1800, although unmarked, is stated to be by this firm (pl. 35).

Very little of the history of this firm has been recorded, but they are now known to have issued a series of American views including the Court House and the Exchange, both in Baltimore, and the Dam and Waterworks at Philadelphia. These views, in an attractive border of fruit and flowers, have hitherto always been illustrated as 'maker unknown'. Some English views in the same border have also been recorded, including one of York Minster (pl. 33). The name of the view is enclosed in a floral cartouche (fig. 27). Neither the English nor American named scenic views ever appear to have been marked with the potter's name. These can now, however, all be attributed to Henshall & Co. on the evidence of a plate with the title 'British Views' (pl. 34) enclosed in the same floral cartouche and having the same fruit and flower border and bearing the rare impressed mark HENSHALL & CO. This firm, who apparently marked very few of their wares, appear to have used the style Henshall & Co. during their whole life, whatever the various partnerships may have been. They evidently took a more important part in the production of underglaze blue transfer-printed wares than has hitherto been recognised, much of which presumably still awaits identification.

Hicks & Meigh of High Street, Shelton. This firm was founded by
Hicks, Meigh & Johnson Richard Hicks, who had been apprenticed as an engraver to Thomas Turner of Caughley. They took over the factory of John & Edward Baddeley in 1806 and made much blue-printed ware, including their own version of the Willow pattern. In 1826 the firm became Hicks, Meigh & Johnson and continued until 1836. They were especially renowned for their good quality ironstone and stone china

---

[*] Jewitt, *op. cit.*, vol. 2, p. 421

(pl. 36). The marks appear with the names in full or the initials H.M. & J. or H.M.J., often with the Royal Arms or a crown. The words 'stone china' and a number are frequently included in the mark. The Royal Arms and Crown marks sometimes appear without the names or initials of the firm (figs. 30 and 31).

Hilditch & Sons   of Church Street Works, Lane End, Longton. Jewitt writes that a firm called Hilditch & Sons took over the Church Street works in 1795, and that their productions followed closely in the wake of Josiah Spode and Thomas Minton. If this is so, they must have produced the early types of blue-printed wares. There is, however, no further record of the firm until they are listed as Hilditch & Martin in 1818.

Hilditch & Martin   This is said to be one of the sons in the above firm trading
Hilditch & Son   in partnership with Martin until 1822, when the style be-
Hilditch & Hopwood   came Hilditch & Son and remained so until 1830, in which year the firm became Hilditch & Hopwood. Ward lists them with two factories in Lane End in 1842. William Hopwood died in 1858, when the works were continued by trustees and were sold in 1867. This firm made china and earthenwares and later on had specialised in elaborately decorated china ware and figures. Even in 1829 Shaw speaks of them as china manufacturers. The mark was H. & S. within a cartouche of various shapes, sometimes surmounted by a bird or crown (figs. 32–34).

Hillcock & Walton   A very rare printed mark recorded by Chaffers. This appears on a blue-printed earthenware dish in the British Museum with a floral pattern and appears to be of the 1830–40 period. In addition it has a printed seal mark with the words 'Semi-China' in the centre (fig. 105) and is identical with the mark commonly seen on an unidentified series with a hop and wheatear pattern border. There is no record of any potters by the name of Hillcock & Walton, and this is possibly the name of the firm for whom the service was made.

Holland, Thomas   of Burslem is listed in 1786 as a maker of black and red china and
Holland, Ann   gilder, and appears again in 1802. In 1818, Ann Holland, possibly his daughter, is listed as of Hill Top, Burslem, and is still so recorded by Ward, about 1842.

Holland & Co. appear in the Burslem list of 1802.

Hollins, T. & J.   of Shelton, Hanley. Two brothers, Thomas and John, started
Hollins, T. J. & R.   potting at some time in the 1790s. At some time before 1818, they admitted their younger brother Richard into partnership and in that year they are listed as T. J. & R. Hollins and must have continued until the end of the 1820s. Shaw lists Hollins as being one of the principal firms in Shelton and Hanley in 1829. Better known for their Wedgwood-type wares, after 1800 they made more general earthenwares, including blue-printed. Impressed marks: T. & J. HOLLINS and T.J. & R. HOLLINS.

Hollins, Samuel of Vale Pleasant, Shelton, another brother of the above firm succeeded his father in 1780. He continued until he retired in 1816, and died in 1820. He also made Wedgwood-type wares, and was for some years a partner in the New Hall China Works, and appears unlikely to have made any transfer-printed wares.

Hughes, Samuel of Lane End, Longton. Jewitt states that Mr Hughes built Daisy Bank Works, Longton, in the latter part of the eighteenth century. This is probably the Samuel Hughes who appears in the Lane End directory in 1802, but who had changed **Hughes, Thomas** to Thomas Hughes by 1818. Shaw mentions a Samuel Jackson Hughes living in Lane End in about 1829, but does not specifically refer to him as a potter.

Hughes, Stephen & Co. of Waterloo Road Works, Cobridge. Jewitt, writing in 1878, said that these works were established in 1820 by Thomas, grandfather of the present Thomas Hughes, and were 'carried on by him and his successors, Stephen Hughes & Co., until about 1856, since when it has been continued solely by the present Thomas Hughes'. Stephen Hughes & Co. are mentioned by Ward in 1842. The *Encyclopaedia of British Pottery and Porcelain Marks* gives the dates as c. 1835–55, which would make the dates of the original firm in the name of Thomas Hughes c. 1820–34.

Hulme, J. & Sons of Waterloo Works, Lane End, appear in Shaw's 1829 list of potters. He remarks that the 'Waterloo factory is well arranged for every purpose, has a flint mill close adjoining and well situated for Coals and Marl'. The life of the firm appears to have been of very short duration. Printed marks HULME & SONS are recorded.

Jackson, Job & John of Churchyard Works, Burslem, began potting in 1831, but went out of business before 1842. Ward in that year lists the works as discontinued. During their short life they issued a long series of American views, some in light blue, but mostly in other colours. They produced some English rural scenes and a few scriptural designs. The borders are various floral arrangements, including bunches of roses, usually encroaching into the well of the plate or dish.

Marks, impressed or printed, may be JACKSON, J. & J. JACKSON or JACKSON'S WARRANTED.

Jackson, Thomas & Co. of Lane End appear in the 1802 list of earthenware potters.

Johnson, Reuben of Miles Bank, Hanley was established by 1818, in which year he appears in the Shelton and Hanley directory, but had ceased to operate by 1842 when Ward records Thomas Furnival (Junr.) & Co., formerly Reuben Johnson. Jewitt refers to the firm as Reuben Johnson & Co. The *Encyclopaedia of British Pottery and Porcelain Marks* states that Reuben Johnson was working from c. 1817–23 and that they were continued by his widow Phoebe Johnson under the style Phoebe Johnson & Son until c. 1838 and cites a mark JOHNSON HANLEY STONE CHINA with a note that it is not certain which potter employed this mark.

Johnson, Ralph of Church Street, Burslem, appears in the 1818 list of potters.

Johnson & Brough of Lane End are listed in 1802. Chaffers states that this firm was succeeded by Benjamin Singleton Brough. Thomas Brough of Green Dock, Lane End, appears in the 1818 list, and may be a continuation of the same firm.

Jones, Elijah of Phoenix Works, Shelton, occupied these works for a year or two only. He was not included in Shaw's list of 1829 and Ward in 1842 lists Joseph Clementson, late Elijah Jones. Clementson (*q.v.*) occupied these works soon after 1832, in the partnership Read & Clementson (*q.v.*), before becoming the sole proprietor about 1839. The approximate dates must have been c. 1830–2.

Jones, Elijah
Jones & Walley
Walley, E. of Villa Pottery, Cobridge, is included in Ward's list of Cobridge potters in about 1841, by which time he appears to have been established for about 10 years. At about this time the firm became Jones & Walley for three or four years, and was then carried on by Edward Walley alone.

Jewitt wrote that the Villa Pottery was carried on by Jones & Walley from about 1835 to 1850 when Edward Walley continued alone until 1865. The *Encyclopaedia*, however, gives revised dates, Jones & Walley 1841–3 with the mark J. & W. which appears on printed marks, often with the name of the pattern included; Edward Walley 1845–56 with an impressed mark IRONSTONE CHINA E. WALLEY

Jones & Beech of Bell Works, Burslem, appear in Ward's list of 1842. Writing of this firm, Jewitt reverses the names and states that part of the Bell Works was taken by Beech & Jones as an earthenware manufactory in 1836, but that in 1839 the partnership was dissolved and Beech carried on alone until 1853, when the style became Beech & Brock. This partnership had lasted for only two years when William Beech carried on alone again, until his death in 1864.

Jones & Son of Hanley. This name appears on blue-printed marks on a series of 'British History' subjects. A vegetable dish and cover, showing scenes at the coronation of Charles II in underglaze blue, has been recorded, on which the elaborate mark included a description of the event. The *Encyclopaedia of British Pottery and Porcelain Marks* gives the dates as c. 1826–28.

The same authority also cites:

Jones, Elijah   of Hall Lane, Hanley, 1828–31
Jones, Elijah   of Mill Street, Shelton, 1847–8.

The name Jones, in lower-case letters, appears on a blue-printed series called 'Egypt'. It is difficult to attribute this mark to any one particular factory, but as they appear to be of the 1830–40 period, it probably refers to Elijah Jones of the Villa Pottery, Cobridge. Printed marks with the initials E.J. also occur and may also refer to this firm.

Keeling, Anthony   of Tunstall. Anthony Keeling occupied the Phoenix Works,
Keeling, A. & E.   Tunstall, at some time before 1780. For a short time, about 1780–1, he was associated with the company of Staffordshire potters who were interested in purchasing Richard Champion's patent. The manufacture of porcelain in this new venture was for a time carried on at Keeling's Tunstall factory, but was soon moved to the New Hall Works at Shelton, when Keeling withdrew from the firm. In 1786 he is listed as a manufacturer of general earthenwares. At some time after this he took his son Enoch into partnership. At a meeting of potters at Burslem in 1795, the firm is listed as Anthony Keeling & Son, but in 1802 the firm appears as A. & E. Keeling, when they worked two potteries in Tunstall. Their trade is said to have suffered during the French wars and Anthony retired in 1810 and the firm came to an end. Anthony Keeling died in 1816.

Keeling, James   of Hanley. The name of Edward Keeling appears in the Hanley directory of 1786. Chaffers states that he was succeeded by James Keeling who is listed in 1802, and again in 1818 as of New Street, Hanley. Further references to him appear in 1823 and 1828. He was a progressive potter who, as early as 1796, invented new processes for the decoration and glazing of pottery, and improvements in kilns and firing processes. Shaw credits him, together with James Gerrard, with introducing improvements in the processes connected with blue-printed pottery. He also mentions that the finest oriental scenery was transferred by him and that, in 1828, he produced dinner services, ornamented with views from the illustrations of Buckingham's *Travels in Mesopotamia*. He was succeeded by S. & J. Burton (*q.v.*) in 1832.

Keeling, Joseph   of Hanley first appears in the 1802 list and remained in operation for only a few years until about 1808. He is best known for his Wedgwood-type black basalt wares, a few of which have been recorded with the impressed mark JOSEPH KEELING.

Keeling, Charles   of Shelton had a short-lived pottery, working from 1822 to 1825: he used the initials C.K. on his printed marks.

76

Keeling, Samuel & Co. of Market Street, Hanley. This firm followed John Glass (*q.v.*) at this pottery in 1840 and is mentioned by Ward at about this time. They made general earthenwares until 1850, when the pottery was taken over by the Meakin brothers. The name in full, or the initials S.K. & CO., appear on a variety of printed marks.

Keeling, Toft & Co. of Hanley. Jewitt states that this firm took over the pottery
Toft & May in Hanley, which had been owned and worked by William
May, Robert Mellor, about 1775. The William Miller appearing in the 1786 list of Hanley potters is very probably a mistake for this man. In 1802 the pottery appears in the name of Mrs Mellor, probably his widow. Three or four years after this the factory was taken over by Keeling, Toft & Co. (called Toft & Keeling by Jewitt). About 1825 the style became Toft & May and is so listed by Shaw. Jewitt says that later it was run for a short time by Robert May alone, until the pottery was taken over by William Ridgway in 1830, as one of the five potteries of which he was the head partner. The Mellors mainly made black basalt wares for the Dutch markets, as did their successors Keeling & Toft, although they branched out into other more general earthenwares. The name is usually impressed in full on recorded pieces. The mark TOFT & MAY is found impressed on blue-printed wares (pl. 67).

Kennedy, James of Commercial Street. Burslem. This man is given in the *Encyclopaedia of British Pottery and Porcelain Marks* as an independent engraver working c. 1818–34 whose signature sometimes appears as part of the design.

Knight, Elkin & Co.
Knight, Elkin & Bridgwood } *see* Elkin, Knight & Bridgwood.
Knight, Elkin & Knight

Lakin & Poole of Hadderidge, Burslem. Thomas Lakin entered
Lakin, Poole & Shrigley into partnership with Poole in 1791. In 1795 Thomas
Poole & Shrigley Shrigley joined the firm, when the style became Lakin, Poole & Shrigley. The following year Lakin disappears from the title and the firm became Poole & Shrigley, but lasted only until the end of 1796.

R. G. Haggar in *English Country Pottery* states that it was John Ellison Poole (1766–1829) who formed the original partnership with Thomas Lakin and that neither of them were potters, the factory being managed by Thomas Heath. This is presumably the Thomas Heath (*q.v.*) who carried on a pottery at Hadderidge, Burslem from 1812 to 1835. Lakin & Poole were extensive manufacturers of general earthenwares, including black basaltes, creamwares and figures. According to Jewitt, some billheads of the firm issued with 'painted wares' in 1792 had been altered by 1793, in ink, to 'printed' wares. It would appear from these invoices of 1792–6 that blue-printed was made in considerable quantities between 1793 and 1796. Recorded marks on various wares are LAKIN & POOLE and L. & P. BURSLEM. The mark POOLE, LAKIN & CO. has been noted on some black basaltes and probably refers to the Shrigley partnership.

Lakin, Thomas & Son of Stoke. This firm operated from about 1810, first as **Lakin, Thomas** Thomas Lakin & Son, and later as Thomas Lakin, but had ceased to work when the 1818 directory was compiled. A blue-printed, shell-shaped dish illustrated by William Turner* with the impressed mark LAKIN and described as having been made by Lakin & Poole is more likely to have been made by Thomas Lakin of Stoke. The view of classical ruins is typical of this period. A similar dish in the Victoria and Albert Museum has the name Lakin impressed in lower-case letters (pl. 40).

Lockett This family had established a pottery at Burslem probably at some time about 1780. Timothy and John Lockett appear as white stone potters in the 1786 Burslem directory. About 1802 the family appear to have moved to Lane End.

Locket, J. & G. are first listed at Lane End in 1802. This name and initials are recorded as an impressed mark.
Locket, John & Co. of King Street, Lane End, appear in the 1818 directory.
Lockett John & Sons are listed at Lane End by Shaw, about 1828.
Lockett, John & Thomas are recorded with two factories at Lane End by Ward in 1841, and afterwards according to Jewitt became John Lockett, who still controlled two factories, one in King Street and the other in Market Street.
It is difficult to establish the precise relationship and dates of these firms, but the *Encyclopaedia of British Pottery and Porcelain Marks* gives the following information:

> J. & G. Lockett, c. 1802–5, subsequently George Lockett & Co.
>
> J. Lockett & Co., c. 1812–89
>
> John Lockett, c. 1821–58, formerly George Lockett
>
> John Lockett & Sons, 1828–35, subsequently John & Thomas Lockett, the first three as of Lane End, the last John Lockett & Sons of Longton.

All these styles appear as impressed or printed marks.

Lockett & Hulme of King Street, Lane End made earthenwares from 1822–6 and used the initials $\begin{smallmatrix} \text{L. \& H.} \\ \text{L.E.} \end{smallmatrix}$ on their printed marks (fig. 35).

Lownds & Beech *see* Beech, James.

---

* W. Turner, *Transfer Printing on Enamels, Porcelain and Pottery*, 1907, pl. XXX, fig. C6

Machin, Joseph of Waterloo Road, Burslem, appears in the directory of 1802, and again in 1818. By 1828 the firm has become Joseph Machin & Co., when Shaw refers to them as having one of the largest potteries in Burslem. Blue-printed wares of this period are found with the mark J.M. & CO. and may well refer to this firm.

Machin & Baggaley of Waterloo Pottery, Burslem. Another Joseph Machin, who appears in the 1802 Burslem list as an enameller, is probably the same Joseph Machin who, according to Jewitt, together with Jacob Baggaley bought the Waterloo Works, Burslem, about 1809, and made china and earthenwares. They are also said to have been important cobalt refiners and colour makers. Joseph Machin died in 1831 and was succeeded by his son William. Two years later Baggaley was replaced by William Wainwright Potts and the firm became Machin & Potts.

Machin & Potts This is the same Potts who, in 1831, had taken out, in conjunction with his partners in a calico printing business at the New Mills Works, near Derby, a patent for a rotary press for printing transfers in a single colour from revolving steel cylinders. In 1833 he joined William Machin and used this new process for printing on china and earthenware. In 1835 W. W. Potts took out a further patent for multi-coloured printing. Ward, writing about 1842, as if the firm still existed, said that Machin & Potts 'have within a few years past introduced a new process for printing china and earthenware by machinery, the paper impressions being thrown off from steel cylinders, each engraved with the required pattern in rapid and almost endless succession, ready for the transferrer's hands'.

Although presumably chiefly occupied as a decorating establishment, this firm were practical potters, and produced their own wares. Printed marks often referred to the patent. Chaffers illustrates an interesting printed mark on a blue-printed plate with 'W. W. POTTS'S PATENT Printed Ware' above a crest and 'St. George's Potteries, New Mills, Derbyshire' below, and was presumably an early piece made whilst experiments were still being made in Derbyshire.

Machin & Thomas of Burslem, makers of printed earthenwares, are listed in the *Encyclopaedia of British Pottery and Porcelain Marks* as c. 1831–2. This was perhaps the style of the two previously quoted firms during a short interval between the Machin & Baggaley and Machin & Potts partnerships.

Maddock & Edwards of Newcastle Street, Burslem. John Maddock was in
Maddock & Seddon partnership with James Edwards (*q.v.*) for a few years prior
Maddock, John to 1839, when the latter left to start his own pottery and the firm became Maddock & Seddon; it is so listed by Ward in 1842. About this time Seddon left the firm and John Maddock carried on alone until 1855, when he took his son into partnership as John Maddock & Son. John Maddock took out a patent in 1846 for improvements in kilns and ovens.

The marks MADDOCK or M. & S. are found, sometimes with the name of the pattern and the type of body.

Mare, John & Richard   were established in Hanley at some time in the 1760s. They both signed the potters' price agreement in 1770, and appear again in the 1786 directory.

Mare, John   In 1802 John Mare alone is listed, and the same name, whether this man or a successor, appears in a list of 1823. The firm evidently came to an end soon after this date, and is not mentioned by Shaw in 1828.

Mare, Matthew & Co.   of Vale Pleasant, Hanley, are listed in the 1818 directory and may well be the style of the firm at that time, as the name of John Mare is omitted.

Fine quality blue-printed earthenwares with the impressed mark MARE are recorded, and probably refer to John Mare.

Marsh, Jacob   appears in the Burslem list of 1802. The same name appears in the 1818 list, but in Lane Delph. Jewitt is probably speaking of the latter when he mentions Mr Marsh of King Street Works, Foley, Fenton, who succeeded Shelley (*see* supplementary list) and preceded T. & J. Carey at these works. His dates would probably be c. 1804–18.

Marsh, Sam   of Brownhills may have succeeded the first Jacob Marsh
Marsh, Samuel & Co.   mentioned above and appears in the 1818 directory. The firm had evidently become Samuel Marsh & Co. when Shaw was writing in 1828.

Marsh & Haywood   of Brownhills are listed in the 1818 directory and continued until some time before 1842, when they were succeeded, according to Jewitt, by G. F. Bowers (*see* supplementary list).

Marsh, John Riley   is mentioned in 1828 by Shaw among an important group of potters who owned the largest potteries in Burslem in which 'we find every kind of Porcelain and Pottery regularly forwarded to all the marts of both continents'. No other record of this potter appears to exist.

Martin, John   of Shelton. Both this name and town are occasionally found engraved as part of the pattern on underglaze blue transfer-printed wares, and is probably the signature of an outside engraver, rather than a master potter. The period appears to be about 1810.

Martin, Shaw & Cope   of Lane End do not appear in the 1818 directory. Possibly
Martin & Cope   this Martin was the partner in Hilditch & Martin (*q.v.*) of Lane End (listed in that year), who withdrew from the firm in 1822, and may then have started his own firm. At some time before 1828 the style became Martin & Cope.

Ward lists Martin of Lane End in 1842 which may have been the ultimate style of the firm.

Mason, Miles   of Lane Delph. As a young man Miles Mason had opened a business in Fenchurch Street, London, importing Chinese porcelain. He obtained some practical potting experience at both the Derby and Worcester porcelain factories. About 1795 he joined Thomas Wolfe and John Lucock, two Staffordshire potters, and took over John Pennington's Islington Pottery in Liverpool, where they made a type of hybrid porcelain. About 1800 Mason left Liverpool and became the proprietor of a small pottery at Lane Delph in Staffordshire. In 1805 he moved to the larger and more modern Minerva Pottery in Lane Delph. Over the next few years he took his three sons into the business: William, the eldest (1785–1855), who left in 1811 to start his own factory; George Miles (1789–1859); and Charles James (1791–1856). Although Miles Mason's chief interest was in porcelain, he made stone china at Lane Delph, mostly Chinese in character, decorated sometimes in underglaze blue (pl. 37) but mostly in rich colours. He retired in 1813 leaving the control of the firm to his two younger sons, and died in 1822. Miles Mason used the impressed mark M. MASON or MILES MASON in full, often accompanied by a square, pseudo-Chinese seal mark. The seal mark sometimes occurs without the name (figs. 36 and 37).

Mason, G. M. & C. J.   of Lane Delph. George Miles and Charles James Mason took over control of the firm on their father's retirement in 1813 and moved to a new pottery. In the same year a patent for the famous 'Ironstone China' was taken out in the name of C. J. Mason. From this time the brothers concentrated on the manufacture of ironstone china, a very hard and heavy material of great strength. Their output of tablewares and other ornamental domestic wares was immense. The decoration was still mainly highly coloured in reds, green and blues, but many specimens of underglaze blue transfer-printing still survive. They are mainly oriental, bird and floral patterns. G. M. Mason retired in 1829 and left C. J. Mason to carry on alone. Marks of this period consisted of the full names and initials of the two brothers, or various forms of printed marks incorporating the words MASON'S PATENT IRONSTONE CHINA. The well-known mark of MASON'S above the crown, with the patent ironstone china wording in the ribbon below, originated during this period (pl. 38).

Mason, Charles James & Co.   of Lane Delph. When George Miles Mason retired from the firm in 1829, his brother Charles James Mason continued as C. J. Mason & Co. making the same type of wares. In 1845 the company was dissolved and C. J. Mason continued the pottery on his own. Various printed marks were used during this period, usually including the full name or initials C.J.M. & CO. The words 'Fenton Stone Works' are often included. An impressed mark MASON'S CAMBRIAN ARGIL referring to a special body appears to be of this period but was probably also used during the G. M. & C. J. Mason partnership (pl. 39).

Mason, Charles James   carried on the firm on his own from 1845, continuing to make the same type of ironstone china and in addition more general types of earthenware. Towards the middle of the century, according to Jewitt, he ran into financial difficulties and sold the patent right, moulds and copper plates in 1848 to Francis Morley. During this period the usual mark was one of the MASON's crown and ribbon type. Francis Morley, and his successors G. L. Ashworth & Bros, continued to use the printed Mason's patent ironstone mark. A mark using the words 'Improved Ironstone China' is said to date from about 1840.

Mason, William of Lane Delph started his own factory when he left his father's firm in 1811. He made general earthenwares and specialised in blue transfer-printed wares, including scenic views. Printed marks W. MASON are recorded, but are rare. In 1824 he closed down his pottery and opened a retail china and earthenware establishment in Manchester.

May, Robert *see* Keeling, Toft & Co.

Mayer is a very old name in its various forms in the history of the Staffordshire Potteries. The first potter of note coming within the period of blue-printed wares was Elijah.

Mayer, Elijah of Cobden Works, Hanley. Elijah Mayer was active in the
Mayer, Elijah & Son potter's trade during the last quarter of the eighteenth century. Although listed as an enameller in 1770, and again in 1786, he was making his own wares at least as early as 1784. He made creamwares, black basaltes and other wares of the Wedgwood type with impressed marks E. MAYER. About 1805 he took his son, Joseph, into partnership when the style of the firm became Elijah Mayer & Son. Although Elijah Mayer died in 1813, the trading name remained E. Mayer & Son until the factory closed about 1833. Shaw in 1829 lists the firm as 'Elijah Mayer & Son (or in fact the son only, the father having died many years ago) which has maintained a very high station in the scale of manufacture, for the excellence of the Queen's Ware and Brown Line Ware there fabricated. But it is now notable for a species of Porcelain manufactured only here.'

Mayer, Joseph & Co. of Church Works, Hanley. Joseph Mayer, in addition to his
Mayer & Co. father's factory (*see* above) also occupied the Church Works, Hanley, in his own name from about 1820, which operated under the name of J. Mayer & Co., or Mayer & Co., until 1831, when the works were rented to William Ridgway. About 1833 he gave up the Cobden Works, also to Ridgway, and ceased to be an active potter: he died in 1860. Marks may be Joseph Mayer & Co. or Mayer & Co.

Mayer, Thomas of Cliff Bank Works, Stoke. Thomas Mayer appears to have acquired this pottery about 1825, and is listed by Shaw who remarks that he was 'a very intelligent potter'. He produced much dark blue-printed ware, including both English and American views. He is especially known in the United States for his series of engravings of the Arms of American States, which are now very rare (pl. 42). The borders are very distinctive, typically composed of vine leaves and trumpet-shaped flowers with a wheel-like device introduced at equidistant intervals, three on plates and four on dishes. Encircling the edge of the piece are overlapping scale motifs, with the central view framed in a lace-like leaf pattern. Thomas Mayer ceased potting at Stoke about 1835 and moved to Longport, near Burslem, but appears to have remained in business there only for a short time, although the name appears in Ward's list of about 1842; but this may apply to the following entry of Mayer Brothers.

Marks may be T. MAYER or T. MAYER, STOKE. Blue-printed wares usually bear a circular impressed mark with T. MAYER STOKE STAFFORDSHIRE in the outer circle, and an eagle, with the word WARRANTED above it, in the centre (fig. 38). A blue-printed eagle also appears, with a ribbon in its mouth bearing the words 'E pluribus unum'. Alternatively these words appear on a scroll beneath the eagle's claws.

Mayer, Thomas, John & Joseph of Dale Hall Pottery, Longport, Burslem. These three brothers followed Joseph Stubbs at these works at some time after 1836. They continued to make the blue-printed wares for which Stubbs is so well-known, but specialised in polychrome printing and more sophisticated wares, including porcelain. The Thomas Mayer in Ward's Longport, Burslem, list of about 1842 probably refers to this firm rather than the firm in the sole name of T. Mayer (*see* above). Marks used were T.J. & J. MAYER or MAYER BROS.

Mayer & Newbold of Market Place, Lane End, began potting just before 1818, in which year they appear in the Lane End directory, and continued until about the mid-1830s. By 1837 Richard Newbold was the sole proprietor. This firm made earthenwares and porcelain. The marks used were Mayer & Newbold in full or the abbreviations MAYᴿ & NEWBᴰ and M. & N., the last sometimes in cursive characters (pl. 41). The descriptions 'Opaque China' or 'New Opaque' are sometimes included.

Meigh, Job
Meigh, J. & Son
Meigh, Charles of Old Hall Pottery, Hanley. Job Meigh is said to have renovated these works during the last decade of the eighteenth century, but no mention of the name is found until 1802, when Meigh & Walthal appear in the Hanley directory. If this is the same firm, Job Meigh had assumed sole control a year or so later and traded as Job Meigh. About 1812 he took his son Charles into partnership and the firm became J. Meigh & Son. The father died in 1817, but the pottery was still listed as J. Meigh & Son by Shaw in 1829. This style remained unchanged until about 1835, when it was altered to Charles Meigh. In 1850 Charles Meigh took his son, another Charles, into the business as Charles Meigh & Son. Except for a brief period in 1851 when the firm became Charles Meigh, Son & Pankhurst, the title remained C. Meigh & Son until 1861, when it was incorporated

as a limited company under the style of Old Hall Earthenware Co. Ltd. Among a great variety of earthenwares, blue-printed was made throughout the life of the firm. When the name of the firm became Charles Meigh, most of the printed wares were made in the then fashionable colour printing. Sets of American views called 'American Cities and Scenery' were made in various colours with a border of small flowers. During the first period of Job Meigh the mark was MEIGH impressed or OLD HALL printed or impressed. After about 1835 marks consisted of names or initials according to the period. Pattern marks usually include the initials C.M. Before 1835 this type of mark bear the initials J.M. & S. Various seal-type marks, sometimes with the type of body in the centre, were used during most of the life of the firm.

Meir, John of Tunstall had a small earthenware pottery in Tunstall by about **Meir, John & Son** 1810 and extended his works when Benjamin Adams gave up his Greengates Pottery, Tunstall about 1820. In 1836 the firm became John Meir & Son and remained in operation until almost the end of the century. Marks are impressed or printed, usually with the initials J.M. and J.M. & S. The J is often printed as I. Blue-printed wares are recorded with the impressed mark MEIR, including small toy sets with nursery rhyme-type prints (pl. 43). William Turner* illustrates a blue-printed dish with pierced openwork rim, and rural scene, stated to be marked F. MEIR. No potter with this initial can be traced and it may be a misreading for I. or J. MEIR. The familiar boat, bridge and river scene was also produced when the firm was John Meir & Son and several marks of this later period include the name of the pattern such as 'Korea', 'COMO', etc.

Mellor, John near the Market Place, Burslem, appears in the 1818 directory. No further trace of this name is found in Burslem until Mellor, Venables & Co. **Mellor, Venables & Co.** were established at Hole House Pottery, Burslem. They are mentioned by Ward as makers of china and earthenware in 1842. The *Encyclopaedia of British Pottery and Porcelain Marks* gives the dates as 1834–51. They made blue-printed wares, but starting at this date much of their transfer-printed work was in colours other than blue. They made a series of American views in various colours, including a light blue. The borders are made up with medallions enclosing coats of arms, festooned with wreaths, connected by bunches of small flowers. Impressed or printed marks of differing design include the name in full, or the initials M.V. & CO.

Mellor, William of Hanley. *See* Keeling, Toft & Co.

Minton, Thomas of Stoke. Thomas Minton was apprenticed as an engraver to Thomas Turner at Caughley, and was later employed by Josiah Spode at his London warehouse to engrave copper plates. In 1789, recognising the increasing demand for blue-printed earthenwares, he left London and established himself as a master en-

* W. Turner, *op. cit.*, pl. XXIX, fig. c.4

graver at Stoke-on-Trent. Here he executed versions of the Willow pattern and other designs adapted from oriental originals for Spode and other potters. In 1793 he joined Joseph Poulson, a practical potter and, with financial assistance from William Pownall, began to make blue-printed on a small scale. At the same time he purchased land at Stoke and started to build a new factory, which came into operation in 1796. The firm traded as Minton & Poulson in the beginning, but, as soon as Pownall was admitted as a sleeping partner, the firm became Minton, Poulson & Pownall. Joseph Poulson died in 1808. In 1817 Thomas Minton's two sons, Thomas and Herbert, were taken into the firm, which became Thomas Minton & Sons. Thomas, the eldest son, left the firm in 1821 and Thomas Minton senior died in 1836. Herbert Minton then took John Boyle into partnership and the style of the firm from 1836–41 was Minton & Boyle. When John Boyle left the firm in 1841 to join Josiah Wedgwood, the firm became Minton & Co., or alternatively Minton & Hollins after 1845, when Michael Hollins became a partner. Herbert Minton died in 1858. In the early days earthenwares only were made, chiefly blue-printed, including Willow, Broseley, Buffalo and many other patterns imitating Nankin designs. Innumerable other patterns have been issued during the life of the firm, which has continued to the present day. Considering the very large quantities of blue-printed which were issued in the beginning, much of it must have been unmarked, judging from the scarcity of early identifiable pieces. Later, many printed foliated cartouche or ribbon marks were introduced, containing the name or number of the pattern, and the type of body. These nearly always included the name Minton or the initials of the various partnerships, such as M, M. & CO., M. & B., M. & H. *Chinoiserie* patterns remained, throughout, the chief theme of all engravings: no named scenic views appear to have been recorded.

Mist, James   *see* Abbott & Mist.

Morley, Francis & Co.   *see* Ridgway, Morley, Wear & Co.

Mortlock, John   started as a retailer of earthenware and china in London in 1746, and a succession of John Mortlocks, with addresses in Oxford Street, Orchard Street and Portman Square, ran the firm for well over a century: the firm continued under the name of Mortlocks until 1933. They held agencies for many manufacturing potteries and ran a decorating establishment at their Pottery Galleries for wares bought in the white. About 1807 they were appointed London agents for Haynes, Dillwyn & Co. of the Cambrian Pottery, Swansea. Other agencies were held for Coalport, the Brameld pottery at Rockingham and Minton's. Early wares of these firms may, very rarely, be found with the impressed name Mortlock; later, printed marks occur. The small blue-printed Willow pattern plate illustrated (pl. 84) with the printed name and addresses of the firm on the front and the name of their representative, Mr Narracott, on the back, was evidently used as a trade card and was probably made at Swansea (pl. 85).

Moseley, John of Cobridge and Burslem. John Moseley appears in the 1802 directory at Cobridge. In 1818, two entries show that he was working two potteries, one at Cobridge and the other at the Churchyard Works, Burslem. Jewitt states that these Burslem works were occupied by Moseley after Thomas Green (*q.v.*) went bankrupt in 1811. The *Encyclopaedia of British Pottery and Porcelain Marks* says that prior to 1802 Moseley was in a partnership, Moseley & Dale, perhaps the same Dale who was for a short time in partnership with Ralph Stevenson of Cobridge. The impressed mark MOSELEY appears on earthenwares of the Wedgwood type. It is most unlikely that blue-printed wares were not made at one of Moseley's potteries during the first 20 years of the nineteenth century.

Moseley, William of Queen Street, Black Works, Burslem, appears in the 1818 directory.

Myatt, Joseph of The Foley, close to Lane Delph, Fenton, appears in the 1802 directory. The entry of Ben & Joseph Myatt of Lane End in the 1818 directory probably relates to a continuation of the same pottery. Shaw, writing in 1829, refers to the late Mr Myatt, almost certainly meaning Joseph Myatt, and infers that he was working as early as 1790. The life of the firm, therefore, appears to be c. 1790–1825. Jewitt states that Joseph Myatt made white and printed earthenware and red ware. The impressed name MYATT has been recorded on various wares and may refer to this firm.

Myatt, Ben is listed as having a pottery in his sole name at Red Street, Tunstall, in 1818.

Neale, James of Church Works, Hanley. James Neale had been the London
Neale & Co. partner of Humphrey Palmer, who managed the Hanley works
Neale & Wilson until 1778. In this year, Palmer became involved in financial difficulties and withdrew from the partnership. Neale left London, and took over control of the factory. About 1780 Neale took Robert Wilson, who had been Palmer's works manager, as a partner. The firm is listed as Neale & Wilson in 1786. Between 1788 and 1795 others were taken into partnership, and the firm traded variously as Neale & Wilson, Neale, Maidment & Bailey and Neale & Bailey, or more usually as Neale & Co. The Neale, Maidment & Bailey and Neale & Bailey probably applied only to the London showrooms end of the business. In 1795 Neale appears to have withdrawn from the Hanley pottery, which was taken over by Robert Wilson (*q.v.*). The firm made a wide range of earthenwares, mostly of the Wedgwood type.

Thomas Rothwell (*q.v.*), a decorator of pottery and engraver, worked for Palmer until his bankruptcy in 1778. He remained with Neale & Co. until some time in the late 1780s and then went to Swansea where he produced many copper plates for underglaze blue printing.

Newbold, Richard *see* Mayer & Newbold.

Operative Union Pottery High Street, Burslem. In the Victoria and Albert Museum, a small plate the rims of which are decorated with moulded patterns, including clasped hands, is printed in blue with a beehive device and the words 'Perseverance and Integrity—Society of Operative Potters, High Street Burslem' (pl. 44). It bears an impressed mark OPERATIVE UNION POTTERY and is labelled by the Museum Authorities as c. 1830. Jewitt, in recording the High Street Pottery, Burslem, states that it was 'usually known as "Union Bank", through its having been for some time worked by the Potters' Trades Union, and belonged at one time to a family named Marsh'.* This may refer to John Riley Marsh, listed by Shaw at Burslem in 1828. Pieces bearing similar decoration to the plate, which presumably had been adopted by the Trades Union potters as their crest and motto, were probably issued in large quantities as a form of advertisement. Other transfer-printed patterns were doubtless issued, but have not, so far, been recorded. No other information of the duration of this venture appears to be available.

Pearson The *Encyclopaedia of British Pottery and Porcelain Marks* reports an impressed mark R. PEARSON on blue-printed wares, but no potter of this name with the initial R can be traced. Those traced are:

Pearson, John of Burslem, c. 1830–6
Pearson, Edward of Burslem, c. 1850–4
Pearson, Edward of Cobridge, c. 1853–73.

   Jewitt notes the Abbey Pottery, Cobridge, occupied by 'H. Meakin late Edward Pearson'. Henry Meakin took over the Abbey Pottery in 1873. G. W. Rhead in *British Pottery Marks* states that Pearson & Handcock occupied the Abbey Pottery, Cobridge, from 1846–72.

Phillips, Edward & George of Longport were making earthenwares in 1822 and are noted as having an extensive manufactory in 1829. In 1834 the pottery stood in the name of George Phillips, and is so listed by Ward in 1843: he continued until 1848. Their blue-printed was well executed in a dark and sometimes flown blue. They made a few American views, including one of Franklin's tomb, and also a series of Eton College for the English market (pl. 47). Besides the more ordinary designs including a Willow pattern (pl. 45), they made an extensive series of fruit and flowers called 'British Flowers', and the usual pastoral scenes (pls. 46a and 46b) (fig. 94). Impressed or blue-printed marks are PHILLIPS LONGPORT, E. & G.P., E. & G. PHILLIPS LONGPORT and later G.P. (fig. 41). The Staffordshire knot appears on some marks (fig. 40). The 'E. & G. PHILLIPS LONGPORT' mark is sometimes surrounded by a floral wreath (fig. 39).

Phillips, W. & J. of Lane End appear in the 1802 list of earthenware potters.

   * Jewitt, *op. cit.*, vol. 2, p. 280

Phillips & Bagster   are stated by Jewitt and Chaffers to have taken the pottery in High Street, Hanley, in 1820 following David Wilson & Sons. These are said to have been Jacob Phillips and John Denton Bagster. This firm had been operating for only a short time when Bagster, according to Jewitt, ran the firm alone until 1828. This is evidently the same factory already noted in Hanley under J. D. Baxter as a maker of blue-printed wares, with a misreading of the name, although it should be noted that the name Bagster appears in the *Belle Vue Papers* in 1823.

Pinder, Thomas   of Burslem. This firm was started by Thomas Pinder in
Pinder, Bourne & Hope   Burslem towards the middle of the nineteenth century.
Pinder, Bourne & Co.   In 1851 the style became Pinder, Bourne & Hope, when they took over the Fountain Place Pottery, Burslem, which had been vacated by the well-known firm of Enoch Wood & Sons in 1846. In 1862 the title was changed to Pinder, Bourne & Co. Although too late, strictly, to come within the early history of blue-printed, some well-printed pieces are found with the initials P.B. & H. Chaffers records a blue-printed sauce-dish on feet in the Sheldon Collection marked PINDER, BOURNE & CO.

Plant, Benjamin   of Lane End, Longton. Very little is known of this potter. He is said to have worked in Lane End from about 1780–1820, but does not appear in the 1786, 1802 or 1818 directories. A rare incised signature mark, B. PLANT LANE END, has been recorded on models of animals, etc.

Podmore, Walker & Co.   of Tunstall. According to Jewitt, G. Podmore, Walker & Co. took over the Unicorn Pottery and Pinnox Works in Tunstall in 1825. This appears to be an error, as all other authorities give the starting date as 1834. Some time later they occupied the Swan Bank Pottery, vacated by Ralph Hall (*q.v.*) in 1849. They are listed by Ward in 1843 as having two factories, at Newfield and Tunstall. The initials P.W. & CO. appear on several printed marks. In 1859 the firm became Wedgwood & Co. when Enoch Wedgwood succeeded the older partnership. The *Encyclopaedia of British Pottery and Porcelain Marks* states that Enoch Wedgwood had been a partner in the original firm from about 1856, and that during the period c. 1856–9 the initials P.W. & W. may occur on the mark. After 1856 the marks WEDGWOOD and WEDGWOOD & CO. were also used. Chaffers illustrates a mark of a Unicorn with WEDGWOOD & CO. on a blue-printed plate; as this includes the words 'Trade Mark' it indicates a date after 1860, when the firm was Wedgwood & Co.

Poole, J. E.
Poole, Lakin & Co.
Poole, Lakin & Shrigley   } *see* Lakin & Poole.
Poole & Shrigley

Poole, Richard of Shelton, Hanley, made earthenwares from about 1790 to 1795 and used an impressed mark R. POOLE.

Potts, William Wainwright was a partner at New Mills Works, near Derby, with Richard Oliver and John Potts in a firm of engravers to calico printers. On 7 September 1831 a patent was taken out in the three names for printing on earthenware by means of revolving steel cylinders. In 1833 W. W. Potts appears to have withdrawn from the Derby firm and joined partnership with William Machin at the Waterloo Pottery, Burslem, when the style of the firm became Machin & Potts (*q.v.*). A rare printed mark incorporating the words 'w. w. POTTS' PATENT Printed Ware St George's Potteries NEW MILLS DERBYSHIRE' on a blue-printed plate is illustrated by Chaffers and was presumably an early piece printed under the new patent in 1831–2 at that address before he joined Machin at Burslem, when the mark became 'Machin & Potts Patent'.

Pratt, Felix of Lane End, Fenton. An old-established family of potters of this name operated in Fenton from some time in the first half of the eighteenth century. There were several generations of Felix Pratts; the first of whom anything is recorded was working from about 1780 to 1815, now best known for the domestic wares and figures in bright high-temperature underglaze colours. In 1818 the directory gives the style as F. & R. Pratt and, with the addition of '& Co.' about 1840, the name remained the same well into the present century. Transfer-printing became a great speciality of this firm, especially in the 1840s, when they first produced services with multi-coloured transfers, copies of well-known pictures: even better known are their much collected pot lids.

Pratt, William of Lane Delph. Another potter of the Pratt family is listed in 1802
Pratt, John as William Pratt of Lane Delph. In 1818 this had changed to John Pratt and was the same when Shaw wrote in 1829. Ward about 1841 gives the firm as John & William Pratt of Middle Fenton, lately called Lane Delph. The pottery was still working when Jewitt wrote in 1878, when the style was John Pratt & Co.

Pratt, Hassall & Gerrard appear in a list of Staffordshire potters in 1823, when the partnership had been formed for about a year. According to Jewitt, the firm started as Pratt & Co. at the Minerva Works, Fenton, at some time after Miles Mason gave up the works in 1816. Pratt was joined by Richard Hassall and Gerrard in 1822. This partnership came to an end in 1834 when Hassall was joined by Thomas Green: Hassall withdrew almost immediately. Green remained, and was joined by Richards, when the firm became Green & Richards (*q.v.*) until 1847.

Printed marks incorporate the initials P.H.G. or P.H. & G.

Radford, Thomas was an engraver employed at the Cockpit Hill Pottery Works, Derby, from about 1760 until the factory closed in 1779, and whose signature appears on some overglaze black prints on their pottery. Here he may have become familiar with the underglaze blue printing carried out by Richard Holdship and his assistant William Underwood, at the Derby Porcelain Works. Subsequently he worked for William Greatbach of Fenton, and later for J. & E. Baddeley of Shelton. Shaw states that John Baddeley of Shelton employed Thomas Radford 'to print Tea Services by an improved method of transferring the impression to the bisquet ware; which was attempted to be kept secret but was soon developed; and the glaze prevented the beautiful appearance which attached to the Black printed'.* This must refer to the Baddeleys' early experiments in underglaze blue printing. The name Thomas Radford appears on the 1802 list as an independent engraver at Shelton.

Ratcliffe, William of New Hall Works, Shelton. These works, having been closed for some time after the manufacture of porcelain had ceased, were reopened by William Ratcliffe for the manufacture of earthenwares in 1831. About 1842 they passed into the hands of William and Thomas Hackwood (*q.v.*). Ratcliffe, for no very obvious reason, marked some of his white and printed wares $\frac{R}{HACKWOOD}$, either printed or impressed, possibly because of some financial backing by the Hackwoods. Another mark printed in underglaze blue is shown in fig. 42 and pl. 48.

Rathbone, W. S. & I. of Tunstall appear in the 1818 list of manufactories of earthenware. Shaw mentions a manufactory of considerable extent in Tunstall by the name of S. & J. Rathbone in 1829, possibly a continuation of the same firm. Ward in 1843 lists Rathbone & Brummitt as makers of china and earthenwares.

Read & Clementson of Hanley. Jewitt states that a partnership in these names began in 1832, but that Joseph Clementson (*q.v.*) shortly after became the sole proprietor. This was in fact about 1839. The *Encyclopaedia of British Pottery and Porcelain Marks* gives two short partnerships:

> Read & Clementson, 1833–5
> Read, Clementson & Anderson, c. 1836

and records the printed marks R. & C. and R.C. & A.

Ridgway, Job & George of Bell Works, Shelton, c. 1792–1802. These two brothers were the first of an important family of potters in the history of the production of blue-printed earthenwares. They founded their pottery about 1792, and are said to have prospered as early makers of blue-printed. They appear in the 1802 list of Shelton potters although, in this year, they are said to have separated; George, of

* Shaw, *op. cit.*, p. 213

whom little more is recorded, stayed on at the Bell Works, while Job moved to the Cauldon Place Works, Shelton.

Ridgway, Job of Cauldon Place Works, Shelton, c. 1802–8. On parting from his brother, George, Job Ridgway set himself up at Cauldon Place, Shelton and remained the sole proprietor until about 1808. His blue-printed wares are likely to be mainly of the early pseudo-Chinese pattern. An early printed mark R within a square Chinese-style seal is attributed to him, but could equally well apply to the partnership of the two brothers, Job and George (fig. 47). Probably the majority of pieces were unmarked.

Ridgway, Job & Sons of Cauldon Place Works, Shelton, c. 1808–13. About 1808 Job Ridgway took his two sons, John (1786–1860) and William (1787–1865) into partnership, when the firm became Job Ridgway & Sons which lasted until 1813, when the father died. If marked, wares would have RIDGWAY & SONS impressed or printed.

Ridgway, John & William of Cauldon Place and Bell Works, Shelton, Hanley, 1814–30. After the death of their father in 1813 the two brothers John and William not only continued at the Cauldon Place Works, but also acquired the Bell Works from their uncle, George Ridgway. They carried on making a great variety of earthenwares and china until they dissolved their partnership in 1830. This was the period when the most sought-after examples of Ridgway blue-printed wares were made. They made a series of 'Beauties of America', each engraving showing an important building: they were framed in a border of medallions, each containing a conventional rose. Best known in Britain is a series of Oxford and Cambridge colleges and other buildings: these views are enclosed in octagonal frames with a border of a trailing convolvulus, quartered by medallions containing cherubs feeding and milking goats (pls. 50 and 51). They avoided the then fashionable very dark blue and used instead a mixture of pale and medium colour blue. This Oxbridge series is perhaps technically the most perfect transfer-printing in underglaze blue of all time. A blue-printed mark of an elaborate cartouche contains the name of the scene with OPAQUE CHINA above, and J. & W. RIDGWAY below (fig. 49). Many other patterns were made, including floral designs and rural scenery, and are usually marked, in addition to the name of the pattern, with the initials J.W.R. or J. & W.R. or the name in full. Two other printed cartouche and wreath marks used to contain the view or pattern names are illustrated (fig. 48 and 50).

Ridgway, John of Cauldon Place Works, Shelton, Hanley, 1830–c. 1840. On the dissolution of partnership with his brother William in 1830, John Ridgway continued at the Cauldon Place Works with various changes of partnership until 1858, when he retired.

Ridgway, John & Co. The '& Co.' was added about 1840 and from 1856 until 1858
    c. 1840–55.   the name of the firm was Ridgway, Bates & Co. Changes in

the style of the firm are shown on marked pieces by the initials or names in full, often accompanied by the name of the pattern. John Ridgway continued to make wares for the American market. Very few of the old medium blue pieces bearing his initials have been recorded. Some new American designs were produced in a light blue, but were mainly in the later underglaze colours of red, brown and black etc. These were enclosed in a rather uninspiring border of large and small five-pointed stars. Two of the many marks used by John Ridgway with or without his initials are illustrated (figs. 106 and 107).

Ridgway, William   At the dissolution of the partnership with his brother John in
      1830–4.   1830, William Ridgway kept the Bell Works. At various times,
and with different partners, he took over several other factories, including the Church Works and Cobden Works formerly belonging to the Mayer family. A cartouche mark used by William Ridgway is illustrated (fig. 52).

Ridgway, William & Co.   The '& Co.' was probably added to the name when
      c. 1834–6   L. J. Abington, a former employee of Joseph Mayer,
joined the firm as a partner. The next change took place when William Ridgway took his son Edward J. Ridgway (1814–96) into partnership about 1836, when the firm became William Ridgway, Son & Co.

Ridgway, William, Son & Co.   William Ridgway retired about 1848 when the
      c. 1836–48   firm became Ridgway & Abington (*see* below).
William Ridgway continued to manufacture for the American market in greater quantities than his brother John. Several American views have been recorded in a light blue, although they were printed in other colours as well. One small group in light blue marked 'Catskill Moss', referring to the border pattern, and c.c. have been identified as William Ridgway's ware. Interesting corroboration of this attribution has been found in a design registration with the c.c. mark taken out by William Ridgway, Son & Co. in 1844* (fig. 51).

Ridgway & Abington   The partners were Edward J. Ridgway and L. J. Abington.
      c. 1848–60
      Marks of all these partnerships are shown by the various initials or names in full.

Ridgway, Morley, Wear & Co.   of Shelton, Hanley. This firm took over the Shelton factory of Hicks, Meigh & Johnson in 1836. This was one of the factories in which William Ridgway was interested, as Morley had married his daughter.

Ridgway & Morley   In 1842 the style changed to Ridgway & Morley until 1844, when Ridgway withdrew and the firm became Francis Morley & Co.

The initials R.M.W. & CO. or R. & M. appear on several different printed marks.

Riley, John & Richard   of Burslem. These two brothers began potting at the Nile

* *Encyclopaedia of British Pottery and Porcelain Marks*, p. 713

Street Works, Burslem. They appear in the directory of Burslem earthenware potters in 1802 and probably started shortly before that date. They rebuilt the Hill Works, Burslem, and moved into them in 1814. The works remained open until about 1828. Shaw states that both brothers died at an early age. When he wrote in 1829, both were dead and it seems that Richard died first, probably about 1823, and John in 1828. Their output of china and earthenwares was very large, a great deal of the latter being blue-printed. Apart from the early pseudo-Chinese designs, including Willow pattern, they made the usual pastoral scenes and romantic ruins. An early service was printed with views after the school of Claude (pl. 52). Although they exported to the United States, they do not appear to have produced any American views. They issued a number of English scenic views with a border of large scrolls, but these have become very scarce. Turner illustrates a jug with a view of Gracefield, Queen's County, Ireland,* a design also used by William Adams. Perhaps a little later, about 1820–5, a series of eastern scenes was issued with a border of leaves and flowers (pl. 54). Other services were decorated with attractive designs of fruit and flowers (pl. 53). The garter or strap and buckle mark, with RILEY'S in the upper part of the strap, and 'semi china' in the centre appears fairly frequently. They were probably the first to use this term to describe their type of earthenware, and also this particular design of mark. The majority of their pieces appear to have been marked, either printed or impressed, and frequently both. Unmarked pieces can sometimes be identified as made by the Rileys by a small impressed stamp resembling a six-petalled Tudor rose, but a very similar type of mark was also used by Swansea. The earlier marks J. & R. RILEY and RILEY'S later became RILEY, perhaps signifying that one of the brothers had died (figs. 44–46).

Rivers, William   of Shelton, Hanley. Some ceramic mark books quote William Rivers of Hanley as an early nineteenth-century cream-coloured earthenware potter. Ward in 1843 refers to Richard Dudson of Hanley, occupying premises previously owned by William Rivers & Co. The 1818 directory gives Rivers & Clews of Hanley, Clews possibly constituting the '& Co.'. The *Encyclopaedia of British Pottery and Porcelain Marks* gives William Rivers of Bedford Row, Shelton, Hanley, earthenware, creamware, etc., c. 1818–22. The impressed mark RIVERS has been recorded on various earthenwares.

Robinson & Wood   of Shelton, Hanley.
Robinson, Wood & Brownfield   of Cobridge Works, Cobridge.
Wood & Brownfield
Brownfield, W.   This firm began as Robinson & Wood in Shelton, Hanley, as makers of earthenwares in 1832. In 1836 Jewitt states that they were joined by Brownfield and took the Cobridge Works vacated by J. & R. Clews in 1834. The firm operated for a short time as Robinson, Wood & Brownfield, until the first-named died and the

---

* William Turner, *op. cit.*, pl. 34, fig. c 16

style became Wood & Brownfield; the firm is so listed by Ward in 1843. In 1850 Wood retired and the pottery passed into the sole name of William Brownfield. Blue-printed wares were made throughout the life of the firm, marked wares bearing the appropriate initials. The initials of William Brownfield sometimes occur in the loops of a Staffordshire knot (fig. 15).

Rogers, John & George   of Dale Hall, Longport, Burslem. These two brothers are said to have built their factory at Dale Hall, Longport, near Burslem, soon after 1780 and were probably in operation by 1784. In the 1786 directory of Burslem earthenware potters they are listed as makers of cream-coloured and china glazed blue-painted wares. By 1802 they were working two potteries in Longport. George Rogers died in 1815, when John Rogers took his son Spencer Rogers into partnership and traded as John Rogers & Son. John Rogers died in 1816, but Spencer Rogers continued to trade **Rogers, John & Son**   under the style of John Rogers & Son until 1842, when the Dale Hall Works were purchased by James Edwards (*q.v.*). It should be noted, however, that in the list of Burslem potters in 1818 the two potteries are entered separately as John Rogers & Son of Longport, and Spencer Rogers of Dale Hall. Ward, writing about 1842, notes that 'Spencer Rogers, still trading as John Rogers & Son, was the oldest existing establishment in Longport'. Some authorities state incorrectly that Spencer Rogers retired in 1829; this may, however, indicate the date at which he gave up his second factory.

The Rogers, throughout the life of the firm, were prolific makers of blue-printed wares, and, the pottery being established at the same time that this form of decoration on earthenwares was just beginning to emerge from the experimental stage, they must have been early in the field. Their first transfer-printed patterns were the usual *chinoiserie* designs, being especially noted for their Willow and Broseley pattern services. Later they introduced eastern landscape scenes, usually with an animal prominent in the foreground, one with an elephant (pl. 58), another with a stag, etc., all with varying floral borders. They also used Italian scenes, including a view of Tivoli (pl. 57) (fig. 101). English pastoral scenes were issued, a well-known design being of rabbits in a setting of trees with a farmhouse in the background. They also made some delightful but unnamed English scenic views. Among a very varied list of patterns were the usual sentimental themes issued under such titles as 'The Adopted Child', 'Maypole', 'Love in a Village' etc. A plate of the last pattern in the Victoria and Albert Museum has 'Love in a Village. Act 1. Scene 4' printed on the front of the plate with a printed mark on the back 'THE DRAMA' in a wreath and an impressed mark ROGERS (pl. 59).

They had a large export trade with many countries, but very few American scenes have been recorded. These include three different views of Boston State House (pl. 55) and the City Hall, New York, all in a rich dark blue. One of their most striking issues was a series of naval ships, including the battle between the Chesapeake and the Shannon fought off Boston in 1813: these were framed in a slightly incongruous but attractive border of sea-shells and flowering shrubs (pl. 56). The standard of potting and printing is almost invariably very high.

Many pieces by this pottery are unmarked. The usual mark used throughout the life of the firm was ROGERS impressed. ROGERS & SON and J.R.S. have also been recorded. The mark was sometimes accompanied by the sign for Iron or Mars (fig. 53). Occasionally this device appears alone and can, fairly safely, be attributed to this firm.

Rothwell, Thomas   was born in Liverpool in 1740. Speaking of the year 1767 Shaw writes: 'About this time Rothwell, possessed of great skill as an enameller, engraver and printer, was employed by Mr. Palmer, at Hanley.'* After Humphrey Palmer's bankruptcy in 1778 Rothwell is said to have stayed on for some time with the firm, which then became Neale & Co. (*q.v.*). A few signed overglaze transfer-prints on creamware are recorded which may relate to the period when he was employed by Palmer. By 1790, Rothwell was living at Swansea where he is said to have been responsible for producing most of the early transfer patterns, both overglaze and under-glaze, at the Cambrian Pottery.† An interesting paper by Norman Stretton‡ gives many more details of the life and work of Thomas Rothwell from which it appears that he was living at various times in London and Birmingham. He died at the latter place in 1807. It is probable that for much of his life he was an independent engraver.

Shaw   There have been many Staffordshire potters of this name. The only one to appear in the 1802 directory was in Lane End, but without an initial. Shaw lists both A. Shaw and J. Shaw in Lane End c. 1828. Jewitt mentions that Ralph Shaw built the Victoria Works in Longton about 1828 and worked until about 1853. The *Encyclopaedia of British Pottery and Porcelain Marks* cites a mid-nineteenth-century printed earthenware dish with the mark C. & J. SHAW JUNR, but without being able to trace any potters of this name.

Shorthose   of Hanley. Potters of the name of Shorthose were operating in
Shorthose, John   these styles from about 1780 until 1823. Whether they were
Shorthose & Heath   separate firms or the same firm under different titles is not clear. A John Shorthose is said to have been in business by 1783. In 1802 the firm is listed as Heath & Shorthose, the names presumably reversed in error as the usual mark is Shorthose and Heath, either impressed or printed. In the same year a John Shorthose is also listed as a general merchant in earthenwares in High Street, Hanley. In 1818 the pottery is listed under the sole name of John Shorthose. In 1823 the firm appears in the *Belle Vue Papers* as 'T. Shorthose or assignees', when the pottery presumably closed down. A varied output of earthenware bears the impressed or

* Shaw, *op. cit.*, p. 192
† E. Morton Nance, *The Pottery and Porcelain of Swansea and Nantgarw*, pp. 477–9
‡ *E.C.C. Trans.*, vol. 6, part 3, 1967, pp. 249 *et seq.*

printed marks SHORTHOSE, SHORTHOSE & CO. and SHORTHOSE & HEATH. Blue-printed wares are recorded. Some authorities attribute the impressed letter S with or without an arrow to this pottery (figs. 54 and 55).

Smith, Ambrose & Co. of Burslem. This firm is listed as makers of cream-coloured ware, china glazed and blue-painted in 1786 and may have been among the early makers of blue-printed. Printed and impressed marks A.S. & CO. are recorded.

Sneyd, Thomas of Hanley. This pottery receives passing notice in many pottery books, but with very few particulars. The *Encyclopaedia of British Pottery and Porcelain Marks* gives Sneyd & Hill as the original style c. 1845, followed by Thomas Sneyd 1846–7. Thomas Sneyd is said to have made transfer-printed wares, but at this late date they are likely to have been in colours other than blue. Impressed mark T. SNEYD or SNEYD HANLEY.

Spode, Josiah of Stoke-on-Trent. The first Josiah Spode was born in 1733 and was apprenticed to Thomas Whieldon in 1749. His career on leaving Whieldon is somewhat obscure, but he is said to have purchased a pottery in Stoke in 1776. William Copeland, traveller and manager of Spode's London warehouse, was later taken into partnership when the London end of the business traded first as Spode & Copeland and later as Spode, Son & Copeland. Josiah Spode I died in 1797 and was succeeded by his son Josiah II who left London and took control of the Stoke works until he died in 1827. He, in turn, was succeeded by his son Josiah III, but he died two years later in 1829. The firm was then carried on by W. T. Copeland, son of William Copeland who had died in 1826. In 1833 W. T. Copeland bought the firm outright from the executors of Josiah III and taking Thomas Garrett, his London agent, into partnership the style became Copeland & Garrett until 1847 when Garrett retired and the firm, which still flourishes, continued under the name of W. T. Copeland.

The first Josiah Spode was one of the early pioneers of blue-printed earthenwares in Staffordshire. In 1783 he employed Thomas Lucas, an engraver, and James Richards, a printer, both from Caughley. He is said to have been completely successful in producing underglaze blue transfer-printed wares by 1784, being the first to do so in Stoke, and made it almost to the exclusion of other types of earthenware. When he died in 1797 his son Josiah II continued to make blue-printed on an even larger scale, introducing over the years a large number of new patterns. But he was not so conservative as his father and branched out into other types of pottery, including porcelain just before 1800.

The earliest Spode patterns were the usual *chinoiserie* designs printed in the early style, many of which were engraved by Thomas Minton. These include variations of the Willow and Broseley patterns and another called 'Buffalo' (pl. 31). At first a pearl ware-type body was used, both body and glaze being progressively improved.

About 1805 Josiah II introduced his new 'stone china' body, a heavier and stronger ware: from then on, many new types of earthenware bodies were produced. Josiah II was also responsible for a long list of new and original patterns, beginning probably as early as 1805, with his Italianate series including such designs as 'Castle' (pl. 60), 'Tiber', 'Tower', 'Lucano' (pl. 61) and 'Blue Italian' patterns. Another set of Caramanian patterns were views, mainly in Asia Minor. A new and novel departure, soon after 1810, was the 'Indian Sporting' series, being illustrations of 'Field Sports' such as bear, buffalo, leopard, deer and wolf hunting (pl. 62). Other designs include direct copies of imported Chinese K'ang Hsi blue and white porcelain, the usual pastoral scenes such as 'The Milkmaid', 'The Woodman' and 'Girl at the Well' and many other general designs. A series of 'botanical flowers' similar to those produced by Wedgwood about 1825, are especially attractive.

Spode's earliest blue-printed is difficult to recognise, as few pieces appear to have been marked. The usual mark is SPODE, in either upper or lower case letters, impressed or printed. Most authorities incline to the view that the lower case mark is the earlier, although one apparently early mark is impressed in large roughly formed irregular capital letters. Quite often SPODE is impressed and printed on the same piece. Rare examples have been noted with 'Spode' hand-painted in blue. Occasionally the impressed or printed mark of a cross within a circle occurs (fig. 58), but this is found mainly on early porcelain.* The printed name is usually accompanied by a letter, and the impressed name by a numeral. The earlier examples of the 'Indian Sporting' series often have the title of the scene printed on the bottom in large letters (fig. 57). This was also done at a later date by Copeland & Garrett, but invariably with their impressed mark in addition. Another mark seen on this series is 'Oriental Sports' on a ribbon decorated with roses and thistles, surmounted by a crown. A mark probably used from about 1810 onwards is the name SPODE printed in the middle of a Chinese-type seal (fig. 56): sometimes only half the seal appears below the name. 'Spode & Copeland' or 'Spode, Son & Copeland' and later 'Spode, Copeland & Son' indicates the London warehouse and would date a piece between about 1784 and 1826, but it is doubtful if these marks appeared on any blue-printed earthenwares. Between 1833 and 1847, when the firm was Copeland & Garrett, some good scenic views in borders of leaves and scrolls were produced. The usual printed mark on these was 'Copeland & Garrett' in a circle with 'late Spode' in the centre and name of the scene, e.g. 'A View in Venice'. Another mark consisted of only the initials 'C. & G.' usually in a printed design. A further mark of this period on blue-printed wares, including re-issues of several of the early Spode patterns, was 'COPELAND & GARRETT' in circular form below a crown, with the name of the body 'NEW FAYENCE' in the centre (pl. 63).

After 1847, when the firm became W. T. Copeland, the marks often incorporated the name 'Spode', a practice which has continued until the present day.

* This may be only a workman's tally mark, but appears to be almost peculiar to this factory. A printed cross often appears without the circle

Steel, Daniel of Burslem was established soon after 1786. In 1802 he was occupying the Scotia Works and by 1821 had moved to Nile Street, where he is described as a jasper and ornamental earthenware maker. The works closed down in 1824. Best known for his Wedgwood-type wares, he was also interested in the new printing techniques. Shaw* describes how he obtained his early knowledge of the glue-bat-printing process from William Adams of Cobridge. The name 'STEEL' and 'STEEL BURSLEM' appear as impressed marks.

Stevenson, Andrew of Cobridge. Stevenson's pottery is stated by Jewitt to have been erected in 1808 and worked for a few years under the style of Bucknall & Stevenson (sometimes recorded as Stevenson & Bucknall). Later Bucknall retired, and from about 1816 until 1830 Andrew Stevenson was the sole proprietor. A maker of general earthenwares, he produced large quantities of blue-printed. He exported on a large scale to America and issued over 20 American views, some 12 of which were engraved after drawings by W. G. Wall, an Irish artist, commissioned by Stevenson to go to the United States for this purpose. He also issued a long list of English views, mainly of stately homes. Both American and English scenes were in a medium dark blue.

In addition to these pictorial series, the usual more general patterns including pastoral subjects (pl. 64) were printed in both light and medium tones of blue. Borders were various arrangements of foliage and flowers, notably roses, sometimes with scrolls introduced. Rather incongruously, some of the borders on English views were interrupted by two or four American portrait medallions at the top, and a small American view at the bottom.

The mark used as an impressed stamp 'STEVENSON' or 'A. STEVENSON' or more usually a circular impressed stamp with a crown in the centre surrounded by 'A. STEVENSON WARRANTED STAFFORDSHIRE' (fig. 59). This mark sometimes appears with a further printed mark of an eagle holding a tablet or alternatively an urn festooned with drapery on which is printed the name of the view. Another mark commonly found on the more general designs is an impressed ship with 'STEVENSON' above it (fig. 60). This mark, formerly attributed to Ralph Stevenson, is now generally considered to belong to Andrew. J. A. Fleming† gives this mark for James Stevenson & Co. of the Greenock Pottery in Scotland (*see also* fig. 61).

Stevenson, Ralph of Cobridge. A firm trading as Stevenson & Dale appears in the 1802 Cobridge directory and early writers assume this to be the same pottery which, about 1810, was being worked by Ralph Stevenson alone. About the middle of the 1820s he was joined for a time, possibly for financial reasons, by A. L. Williams. This can only have been a short-lived partnership, as Shaw writing about 1828 refers to R. Stevenson alone. In the early 1830s Stevenson was joined by his son, when they traded as Ralph Stevenson & Son and continued until some time between 1835 and 1840.

* Shaw, *op. cit.,* p. 212
† J. A. Fleming, *Scottish Pottery,* 1923, p. 211

Ralph Stevenson produced a notable series of American views with an attractive border of vine leaves: these are claimed by American writers as the best-executed designs of their buildings and views. He also issued a set of English views, mostly of stately homes, including Windsor Castle. These are all framed in a very attractive border of oak leaves and acorns. On one of his views of Windsor Castle having this oak leaf border he adopted the same peculiar practice as his brother Andrew Stevenson and placed four American portrait medallions at the top of the border and a view of Rochester Aqueduct Bridge at the bottom. Another short series called 'Panoramic Scenery' sometimes had the name of the view on the back, but on others it was omitted: these had a border of foliage. Stevenson used impressed or printed marks of his full name or initials. During his partnership with Williams the mark changed to R. STEVENSON & WILLIAMS or R.S.W. (figs. 63 and 64). During this period a further extensive series of American views was issued but instead of the original vine leaf border these had the same oak leaf and acorn surround which Stevenson had previously used on his English scenes (pl. 65). A few American portrait pieces were made with a flower and scroll border. Later, when the partnership with Williams was dissolved, Stevenson issued further American views and some more English scenes including a few in a 'British Lakes' series, but these were all mostly in colours other than blue. This also applies to designs issued when the style was R. Stevenson & Son, marked in full or with the initials R.S. & S. An impressed mark attributed to Ralph Stevenson is the name STEVENSON above a crown with 'STAFFORDSHIRE' beneath (fig. 62).

Stirrup, Thomas of Lane End. Shaw mentions the late John Stirrup of Lane End who had been employed as a turner by Adams & Prince and who had married the daughter of John Prince and become opulent with the property he received with her. This may have been the father of Thomas Stirrup who appears in the Lane End directories of earthenware potters in 1802, and again in 1818. Jewitt mentions Peel Pottery, Lane End, Longton, which originally belonged to Mr Stirrup. No information of the type of wares made is available.

Stubbs, Joseph of Dale Hall, Longport, Burslem. All early writers give the first date of Joseph Stubbs as some time in the 1790s, which was probably based on a somewhat ambiguous statement by Jewitt. In 1818 the pottery was occupied by Benjamin Stubbs, probably the father of Joseph. It was not for a year or two after this, c. 1820, that Joseph Stubbs became the proprietor, and continued until his death in 1836. For a few years he took a partner, when the title of the firm was Stubbs & Kent. The *Encyclopaedia of British Pottery and Porcelain Marks* gives the dates of this partnership as c. 1828–30. Stubbs produced a series of over 20 American views with a striking border of flowers and scrolls separated by equidistant eagles, three on plates, and either three or four on dishes (pl. 66). A few English views have been recorded, bordered with foliage and pointed scrolls. Among his more general designs was an attractive arrangement of sea-shells, in a dark blue. Many of his pieces appear to have been unmarked. A plain impressed mark 'STUBBS' on a piece of early appearance could presumably also refer to Benjamin Stubbs. Joseph Stubbs' more usual mark was impressed in circular form with 'Joseph Stubbs. LONGPORT' in the outer ring, and a six-pointed star in the centre. A similar mark was used by Stubbs & Kent (figs. 65 and 66). A printed cartouche mark used by Stubbs for some of his view names is shown in fig. 102.

Tams
S. Tams & Co.
Tams & Anderson
Tams, Anderson & Tams

A mysterious potter by the name of Tams has left no record except some extremely good examples of blue underglaze transfer-printed earthenware. An old Staffordshire name, it is first mentioned in connection with ceramics when William Tams of Shelton was employed at the equally obscure porcelain factory at Limehouse, London, at some time between 1745 and 1748*: after the latter date he may have worked at the Longton Hall china factory in Staffordshire. No further mention of the name appears in any of the directories, or other Staffordshire records, until well after the middle of the nineteenth century when two firms, Tams & Lowe of St Gregory's Pottery, c. 1865, and John Tams of Crown Pottery, c. 1875, were both operating in Longton. Neither Shaw nor Ward mentions the name in their histories of the Staffordshire Potteries. One mark book, as if determined to include the right dates, gives John Tams of Longton as 1774–1903.

Blue-printed pieces recorded bear impressed or printed marks TAMS, S. TAMS & CO., TAMS & ANDERSON and TAMS, ANDERSON & TAMS. They are printed in a very rich deep blue, and have a similar type of border, framing the picture with a mass of trees and foliage, used at an early period by William Adams of Stoke. Both these features and the general appearance of the surviving examples point to an early date between 1815 and 1830: they have a fine thick, lustrous glaze.

The very few American views recorded have the tree border and are marked S. TAMS & CO. Of the five home views recorded, four are in London, namely Drury Lane Theatre (pl. 71), the Opera House, the Royal Exchange and Somerset House: the last one is of the Post Office, Dublin (pl. 70) which includes the now demolished Nelson Column. All these views have the tree border encroaching into the well of the dish or plate.

American writers have recorded some later commemorative portrait plates of General Harrison and Henry Clay, in a light blue, made as a special order by John Tams of Longton about 1840, but without quoting any authority for the statement.

Impressed marks may take any of the forms listed above. English views, if marked, usually have a large heavily printed stamp bearing the name of the view and the words 'semi-china' in addition to the impressed name. The view of Dublin Post Office has the printed stamp (fig. 71) and a circular impressed mark TAMS, ANDERSON &

* *E.C.C. Trans.*, vol. 5, part 3, p. 134

TAMS – – – – POTTERY. The word before 'pottery' is illegible and might, on a clear impression, give a clue as to the whereabouts of the factory. Although existing data appear to point to an early Longton pottery, it must remain a matter of doubt whether this firm was operating in Staffordshire or elsewhere, until further evidence is available.

Taylor, George of Hanley. A little-known potter of this name began potting at some time before 1786, in which year he appears in the Hanley list of earthenware potters. He appears again in 1802, but by 1818 the firm, if it is the same one, had become T. & J. Taylor. Shaw about 1828 refers only to T. Taylor in Hanley, but by 1830 the pottery had been taken over by William Ridgway.

Till, Thomas   *see* Barker, Sutton & Till.

Tittensor, Charles of Shelton. Earthenware figures appear with the impressed mark TITTENSOR, but little else is known of him. The *Encyclopaedia of British Pottery and Porcelain Marks* states that he made printed earthenwares on which the printed name-mark appears and gives the dates as c. 1815–23. Possibly Jewitt is referring to the same man when, speaking of the New Hall porcelain factory of Shelton, Hanley, he says: 'In 1825 the entire stock of the concern, which had for a short time been carried on for the firm by a person named Tittensor, was sold off, and the manufacture of china of any description entirely ceased at New Hall.'

Toft & May   *see* Keeling, Toft & Co.

Turner, John of Lane End, Longton. John Turner served a short apprenticeship
   1738–87   to Daniel Bird, a potter making Whieldon-type wares. After a short partnership in a pottery at Stoke, he moved to Lane End in 1759 and began potting on his own. He took Andrew Abbott into partnership about 1781, when the style of the firm became Turner & Abbott.
Turner & Abbott   Although Abbott was probably a practical potter, he appears to have spent his whole time in charge of the London decorating and retail establishment. Later, when he severed his connection with the Turners, he remained at the London showrooms in partnership with James Mist (*see* Abbott & Mist). John Turner died in December 1787 and the Lane End pottery was left to his two sons William (1762–1835) and John (1766–1824). They maintained their interest in the London business with Abbott until 1792, when they dissolved the partnership, although after this date Abbott still continued to act as their London selling agent. William and John Turner appear to have run into financial difficulties soon after their father's death, mainly owing to the French wars.

Turner & Co. In 1803 John Glover and Charles Simpson were taken into partnership, when the style of the firm was Turner & Co. In 1804 John Turner withdrew from the partnership and became manager at the factory of Thomas Minton. In March 1806 Glover & Simpson dissolved the partnership and William Turner carried on alone until he was declared bankrupt later in the same year. In April 1806 Turner's Pottery was advertised to be let and in 1809 was taken over by Richard Woolley (*q.v.*). According to most authorities this was the end of William Turner as a potter, but Bevis Hillier,* in a very detailed study of the Turner family, shows that he did in fact carry on until 1829. In the 1802 directory John and William Turner are shown as having two factories, so presumably in spite of his bankruptcy, William Turner must have been enabled to start again at his second pottery. This is amply confirmed by other sources. An advertisement of a sale in June 1807 speaks of the 'highly reputed manufacture of Messrs. Turner & Co. of Lane End' and goes on to say: 'The Purchasers will also have an opportunity of matching and continuing the patterns, at Mr. William Turner's *present* Manufactory, in Lane End.'† Another advertisement on 12 December 1829 says that an 'Excellent Stock of Earthenware, Potters' Utensils, Copper-plate Engravings, etc. will be sold by Auction upon the Premises, at the Manufactory in High Street, Lane End; the property of Mr. William Turner, who is declining the Potting Business'.‡ William Turner must have weathered his bankruptcy quite successfully, as Shaw, writing towards the end of the 1820s, says: 'In the High Street is the Manufactory of Mr. W. Turner; doubtless one of the most experienced manufacturers which have lived in the district. Indeed we know not of any other who will bear placing along with E. Wood and T. Minton Esqs.'§

The Turners are known to have produced large quantities of blue-printed wares. Shaw states that the elder John Turner employed William Underwood, a blue printer from Worcester, about 1784 and this is presumably the same man who was Richard Holdship's assistant when he undertook to introduce transfer printing to the Derby porcelain factory in 1764. Although John Turner Senior is credited with being one of the first to use the underglaze blue printing technique in Staffordshire, it is questionable whether he did produce very much before his death in 1787. He was a contemporary and great friend of Josiah Wedgwood, and is likely to have had the same feelings as that potter about the aesthetic merit of this new type of decoration. He was probably too interested in his experiments with porcelain and his jasper, basaltes and stonewares to have had a great deal of time for blue-printed. He did, however, make some of the early-type pseudo-Chinese designs including a Willow pattern. Speaking of this, Shaw writes: 'The Pattern Mr. Turner used was the willow *designed by him* from two oriental Plates, still preserved, and exhibited to the Author by Mr. W. Turner.'‖ From

* *Master Potters of the Industrial Revolution. The Turners of Lane End*, 1965
† B. Hillier, *op. cit.*, p. 74
‡ B. Hillier, *op. cit.*, p. 75
§ Shaw, *op. cit.*, pp. 75–6
‖ Shaw, *op. cit.*, p. 214

this, Bevis Hillier suggests the interesting theory that John Turner may have been the artist responsible for producing some of his own designs for the copper plate engravings.

After the father's death, his sons must have turned their attention to blue-printed to a much larger extent. They continued to use *chinoiserie* designs and many more general patterns. The sale in 1829 included copper plate engravings, mentioning Willow, Broseley, village, bird, windmill, temple, sprig, lady-day, shepherd and villager patterns, as well as 4,000 dozen of blue-printed table and tea ware. Some of the marked pieces have perforated rims and embossed wicker work borders (pl. 69). An interesting unmarked plate with an early style engraving of 'The Archery Lesson' (pl. 68) is an almost exact copy of one of the Turners' most common and successful reliefs on their fine moulded stonewares. A jug with this relief pattern with a silver mount dated 1794 is illustrated by Bevis Hillier.* The blue-printed plate is almost certainly by the same potter and made at an early date before the time when stipple printing was combined with line engraving.

The usual mark throughout the life of the factory was TURNER impressed, or possibly I. TURNER in the earliest period. TURNER & CO. would refer to the 1803–6 period, when Glover and Simpson were partners. In 1784, Turner & Abbott were appointed potters to the Prince of Wales, and a printed or impressed mark, with the Prince of Wales' feathers added, was sometimes used after that date (fig. 67).

Occasionally pieces of blue-printed ware are found with the impressed mark TURNER, with printed marks bearing other names or initials, which presumably were bought up at one or other of the public sales by auction. One such case is a series, with a printed mark, called 'Botanical Beauties' with the initials C.R. & S. So far this firm has not been identified.

Twemlow, John   of Shelton. A potter by the name of G. Twemlow was included in the Shelton directory of potters in 1786. Jewitt† quotes from an invoice of goods made by John Twemlow of Shelton in 1797. These are mostly basaltes and some cream-coloured wares. He does not appear on the 1802 list. The initials J.T. have been noted on black basalt ware.

Walker, Thomas   of Lion Works, Sandyford, Tunstall. These works were taken over by Thomas Walker from James Beech in 1845, and continued until about 1856. Ordinary earthenwares were made, including blue-printed, much of which was exported to South America.

Walley, Edward   *see* Jones & Walley.

* B. Hillier, *op. cit.*, pl. 15
† Jewitt, *op. cit.*, vol. 2, p. 311

Warburton   This was an old-established family of Cobridge potters held in high regard for their cream-coloured wares. Jacob Warburton appears in the Cobridge list of 1786.

Warburton, John   of Hot Lane, Cobridge, is listed as having two potteries in 1802. In 1818 the factories, still both in Hot Lane, are listed separately, one in the name of John Warburton and the other James Warburton. Towards the end of the 1820s Shaw lists the firm as Warburton & Co. of Hot Lane, Cobridge (pl. 82).

Warburton, Peter & Francis   of Cobridge. Peter and Francis Warburton are said to have established their pottery in Cobridge towards the end of the eighteenth century. They dissolved the partnership in 1802, when Peter carried on alone until his death in 1813. Francis Warburton went to France and established a pottery at La Charité-sur-Loire.

Wedgwood   The first Josiah Wedgwood (1730–95) began his potting career at a very early age. In 1769 he began the building of the famous Etruria factory, near Burslem. Although he used overglaze printing to decorate his cream-coloured wares to a very large extent, the later method of underglaze printing on earthenwares was never used in his lifetime. After his father's death in 1795, Josiah Wedgwood II took charge of the factory until he retired in 1841, when his eldest son, Josiah III, succeeded him for a short time. In 1844 Francis, younger son of Josiah II, became head of the firm, which with various changes in style still flourishes today.

It is difficult to say when blue printing was first used by the Wedgwood firm, but it was probably not until about 1805, and then only to a limited extent. It was probably between 1825 and 1850 that the use of this type of decoration was considerably increased. This was mostly on a pearl ware body, although a stone-china was used for a time; both had a rich soft glaze. Although the firm exported wares to the United States in considerable quantities, no American views were issued: this also applies to named English scenes. Best known are their shipping and harbour scenes (pl. 73), and Italian landscapes, produced both in blue and brown, and some very attractive floral patterns (pl. 74). The usual rustic patterns were made, of which the one with a church in the background, a cottage on the right with two men talking at a gate, with sheep in the foreground, and a floral border, mainly roses, is typical (pl. 72).

If marked, the name WEDGWOOD, sometimes printed but usually impressed, appears. The three-letter date marks indicate a date after 1860, the third letter indicating the year, beginning with o in 1860.

Marks which can be misleading are:

WEDGWOOD   *see* Wedgwood, Ralph

WEDG WOOD ⎫
J. WEDGWOOD ⎭   *see* Wood, John Wedg

WEDGWOOD & CO.   *see* Ferrybridge Pottery, Yorkshire, also used by Enoch
Wedgwood (*see* Podmore, Walker & Co.)
WEDGEWOOD   *see* William Smith & Co., Stockton-on-Tees, Yorkshire.

Wedgwood, Ralph   of Hill Works, Burslem. Ralph Wedgwood was the son of
1766–1837   Thomas Wedgwood, partner of Josiah Wedgwood at Etruria.
He began potting on his own account at the Hill Works, Burslem, about 1788, but was
unsuccessful, and went bankrupt. He closed the Burslem works in 1796 and became a
partner in the Ferrybridge Pottery, in Yorkshire (*q.v.*). He made earthenwares, but
little is known of the types of ware he produced. If he made any blue-printed at this
early stage it is probable that it would have been marked WEDGWOOD.

Whitehead   An old-established family of Staffordshire potters, and well-known as
makers of salt-glazed wares in the second half of the eighteenth century.

Whitehead, Christopher & Charles   of Shelton appear in the directory of 1786.
Whitehead, James & Charles   sons of Christopher Whitehead, had taken over
control of the factory by 1802, of whom Charles was presumably the surviving partner
as in 1818 the firm appears as 'Executors of Charles Whitehead'.

Williamson
Williamson & Henshall   } *see* Henshall & Co.

Wilson, Robert   of Church Works, Hanley. Robert Wilson was previously in
Wilson, David   partnership with James Neale as Neale & Wilson (*q.v.*). In 1795
Neale had withdrawn and Wilson traded alone until he died in 1801, when his brother
David Wilson became the master potter and is so listed in 1802. About 1815, he took
his sons into the business and traded as David Wilson & Sons. The factory closed about
1818, in which year the directory entry is 'assignees of D. Wilson & Sons'. The firm
made general earthenwares and is best known for figures, lustre ware and cream-
coloured wares. Shaw states that Robert Wilson brought to perfection the type of
pottery known as 'Chalk Body'; 'of very excellent quality for fineness of grain, and
smooth beautiful glaze' and presumably well suited to decoration by transfer-printing.
The mark throughout appears to have been 'WILSON' impressed. Another impressed
mark of a crown with a large C underneath and 'WILSON' below is also attributed to
this firm.

Wolfe, Thomas   of Stoke. Wolfe established a pottery soon after 1780 and was one
of the early Staffordshire potters to use underglaze blue transfer-printing. He appears
in the 1786 directory as a maker of Queen's Ware in general, blue-printed, Egyptian
black, cane, etc.

Wolfe & Co. John Davenport, later to become a very successful potter and prolific maker of blue-printed, started in 1785, first as a workman and later as a partner, with Thomas Wolfe. For a short time the firm was Wolfe & Co.,* but the partnership was dissolved in September 1794, when Davenport started his own factory at Longport. Wolfe carried on a large export business from Liverpool with Ireland, America and the West Indies. He was also a partner in a china factory in Liverpool from 1795–1800.†

Wolfe & Hamilton About 1800, Wolfe's son-in-law Robert Hamilton (*q.v.*) joined him, when the firm became Wolfe & Hamilton, but left to start his own pottery in Stoke in 1811. The pottery reverted to the sole name of Thomas Wolfe until he died in 1818.

The impressed mark 'Wolfe', in lower case letters, appears on early blue-printed Willow-type patterns (pl. 75). An octagonal plate with another version of this pattern is illustrated by G. Woolliscroft Rhead.‡ The impressed mark w has also been attributed to Wolfe, but may apply to other potters, including Enoch Wood and Warburton.

Wood, Enoch of Fountain Place, Burslem. Enoch Wood was apprenticed to
1759–1840   Humphrey Palmer of Hanley and started potting on his own account at Burslem about 1783. In the 1786 list of potters he is shown as working with his cousin, Ralph Wood, who died in 1795. In 1790 James Caldwell was admitted to
Wood, Enoch & Co.   partnership. About this time the firm is shown as Enoch
Wood & Caldwell   Wood & Co., but the usual style of the firm became Wood & Caldwell. In September, 1818 Caldwell retired from the business and Enoch Wood took his three sons Enoch, Joseph and Edward into partnership as Enoch Wood &
Wood, Enoch & Sons   Sons. This was a period of great prosperity for the Wood family and several other potteries were leased to cope with the increasing trade. Enoch Wood died in 1840, but the firm continued as Enoch Wood & Sons until it closed down in 1846.

Enoch Wood is said to have had a large trade with the United States early in the nineteenth century, and is thought to have been the first potter to open up and develop the American market for the underglaze blue-printed scenic wares, soon after the conclusion of the 1812–15 war. American views are recorded with the impressed stamp WOOD & CALDWELL, signifying a date before 1818 (pl. 76). Enoch Wood was certainly the most prolific producer of American views, and was probably the first to introduce the new deep rich blue which became so popular in that country. The great majority of American scenic views have a border of an arrangement of sea-shells and seaweed. These are in two different designs, one with a prominent cockle shell, when the view

* Knowles Boney, *Liverpool Porcelain of the Eighteenth Century*, 1957, p. 134
† B. Watney, *Blue and White Porcelain of the Eighteenth Century*, 1963, p. 75
‡ G. W. Rhead, *British Pottery Marks*, 1910, p. 291

covers the whole of the centre of the dish or plate, and the other, without the cockle shell, when the border encroaches in an irregular pattern into the well of the piece (pl. 80). The latter usually have the name of the scene on the front as part of the decoration, whereas the former have the name on the back as part of a printed mark. Other American borders are floral arrangements (pl. 81), sometimes with scrolls or four reserved medallions. One very ornate border is made up of fruit, berries, foliage and flowers including passion flowers. A few Canadian views were also produced, the recorded pieces all having the shell border.

Enoch Wood was also one of the largest producers of English scenery: only one series of these bear the shell border and these, appropriately enough, were mostly of ports, harbours and other coastal scenes. They include such general titles as 'A Ship of the Line in the Downs' and 'In a Full Breeze'. These have the irregular shaped border pattern and, as in similar borders on American views, usually have the title on the front. Several other series of English scenes were issued. One of these is transfer-printed on the back with 'London Views' and the name of the view in an ornate scroll: they were mainly pictures of buildings in Regent's Park. An exception to this is the very rare one, previously mentioned, of the Bank of England (pl. 77) (fig. 69). This series had a very broad border of fruiting grapevines encroaching far into the well of the piece and coming right up to the central view, which was enclosed in an ornate oblong frame. Another very numerous series was made up of country seats, castles, cathedrals, beauty spots and general views of villages or small towns. These prints filled the whole centre of the piece and were surrounded by a modified version of the grapevine border and included flowers of the convolvulus type. They had such titles on the back as 'Harewood House, Yorkshire', 'Belvoir Castle', 'York Cathedral', 'Guy's Cliff, Warwickshire' (pl. 78) and 'View of Richmond'. The border of another series called 'English Cities' was a completely new departure, and consisted of an elaborate arrangement of flowers and scrolled reserves, reminiscent of the early brocaded patterns. This was a later issue and the scenes were printed in various colours, including a light blue, and generally bear an impressed mark E.W. & S., together with a printed mark of the name of the city on two scrolls, surrounded by a bishop's mitre and staff.

A large number of African and Indian subjects were printed; also a set of Italian scenes bordered with a design of flying cupids among flowers and foliage. A series of about 12 French views were issued, including four of 'La Grange', Lafayette's home in France. These had another version of the grapevine border with foliage and flowers of which a hollyhock is prominent.

Many more general designs (pl. 79) were made; these included floral patterns, a Cupid design and another called 'The Young Philosopher', the last with a flower border in which the rose and passion flower are most conspicuous. Religious subjects, scenes from the New Testament, have such titles as 'Christ and the Woman of Samaria' and have borders of flowers and scrolls.

Exactly how early Enoch Wood began to use underglaze blue printing is difficult to say. There is no reason why it should not have been soon after the founding of the firm and probably not later than 1790. Early unmarked pieces may exist which have not been recorded. Examples are found which are marked WOOD or E. WOOD and this includes some of the American scenes; other marks are ENOCH WOOD & CO. and WOOD & CALDWELL. Some wares marked E.W. or simply W or W(xxx) are attributed to this pottery. An approximate date can only be assigned to examples bearing these marks on stylistic grounds and other features. On more sure ground are those which, forming the large majority, bear the mark E.W. & S. or ENOCH WOOD & SONS: this was the style of the firm after 1818. The latter mark usually took the form of an impressed circular stamp with a spread eagle in the centre with a shield on its breast, encircled by the words E. WOOD & SONS BURSLEM WARRANTED (figs. 68 and 72). An eagle sometimes occurs on a blue-printed mark with a branch in its claws with the words E PLURIBUS UNUM on a scroll flowing from its mouth. The words 'Stone', 'Stone China' or 'Semi China' are sometimes included as part of the mark. 'Celtic China' was the name given to one series, printed in various colours including a light blue, and usually bearing the impressed E.W. & S. mark. A late mark, after the death of Enoch Wood in 1840, may be E. & E. WOOD relating to the surviving partners Enoch and Edward Wood, Joseph having previously withdrawn from the firm. One of the several printed wreath marks used by E. Wood & Sons is illustrated (fig. 70).

Wood, John of Brownhills, Tunstall. John Wood was making earthenwares at Brownhills from about 1782 until he was murdered in 1797. He was followed by his son, also John Wood (1778–1848). In 1818 the firm appears as Wood & Brittell, and in a list of 1823 as Wood & Brettell. Assuming this to be the same firm, Brettell must have dropped out of the partnership within the next few years, as Shaw mentions John Wood only as the master potter of Brownhills in 1828. At about this date Wood was **Wood & Challinor** joined by Edward Challinor (*q.v.*), when the style became Wood & Challinor. About 1831 they began to build a new pottery called Woodlands at Tunstall, which came into operation about 1835. They worked the two potteries in conjunction for a time, but after a few years the Brownhills factory was closed down. The firm is listed as Wood & Challinor of Woodlands by Ward in 1843. This partnership appears to have ended about this time, when John Wood's son, John Wedg Wood, moved from his pottery at Burslem and joined, or took over control of, Woodlands from his father. Blue-printed pieces occur with the initials W. & C. and probably refer to the Wood & Challinor partnership.

Wood, John Wedg of Burslem and Tunstall. The Hadderidge factory at Burslem was let to John Wedg Wood by William Adams of Greenfield soon after 1839 and he was recorded at these works by Ward in 1843. Shortly after this date he appears to have left these works and joined his father at Tunstall. His father John Wood died in

1848, but probably retired before this date. John Wedg Wood appears to have taken control from about 1845 until his death in 1857. Marks used were J. WEDGWOOD or J. WEDG WOOD or WEDG·WOOD. The *Encyclopaedia of British Pottery and Porcelain Marks* attributes an impressed mark W.W. to this firm.

Wood & Brownfield   *see* Robinson, Wood & Brownfield.

Woolley, Richard   of Turner's Pottery, Lane End, Longton. Richard Woolley was originally a partner in Chetham & Woolley of Lane End (*q.v.*). He dissolved the partnership and rented Turner's Pottery in 1809, but became bankrupt in 1814. His mark was WOOLLEY impressed.

Yale & Barker   of Lane End, Longton, are listed by Ward in 1841. J. P. Cushion in *Ceramic Marks* gives the dates as 1841–53 and the marks as Y. & B. The *Encyclopaedia* states that from 1845 to c. 1853 the partnership may have been Yale, Barker & Hall, **Yale, Barker & Hall**   who may have used the mark Y.B. & H.

Yates, John   of Shelton, Hanley. This name first appears as one of the Staffordshire potters who signed a price agreement in 1770. By 1786 a John Yates is listed at both Hanley and Shelton, possibly the same man working two potteries. In 1802 the Hanley firm appears to have become Yates & Shelley while the Shelton pottery is listed in the names John & William Yates. By 1818 only one firm is listed and appears in the sole name of John Yates of Broad Street, Shelton. Shaw in about 1828, by which time Shelton and Hanley had been amalgamated, mentions only J. Yates of Hanley. Ward **Yates & May**   describes the firm as Yates & May in 1843, saying that the firm was previously John & William Yates who had taken over from their father, who presumably was the original John Yates. Shaw* states that the first John Yates had engaged John Ainsworth, an engraver and printer from Caughley, about 1783, and he must be considered, therefore, as one of the first Staffordshire potters to begin producing underglaze blue transfer-printing.

The Shelton pottery appears to have been registered in the sole name of John Yates from some date prior to 1770 until the late 1830s, first the father and then the son, with the exception of the time c. 1802 when it stood in the name of the brothers John and William Yates. An impressed mark YATES, which appears on some wares, is likely to have been used throughout. The initials J.Y. have been recorded on blue-printed earthenwares.

When the firm became Yates & May, at some time before 1841, Ward noted that they were making both china and earthenwares.

The *Encyclopaedia of British Pottery and Porcelain Marks* gives the duration of the John & William Yates partnership as 1795–c. 1813.

* Shaw, *op. cit.*, p. 214

West Country Potteries

Bristol Pottery Bristol

Ring & Co. This pottery was originally a delftware factory and was bought from Richard Frank by Joseph Ring in September 1784. In 1788 Ring took William Taylor and Henry Carter into partnership and traded as Ring & Co., or Ring, Taylor & Co. Ring was accidentally killed in the same year, but his widow carried on under the same style until 1813. In that year a new partnership was drawn up between Henry Carter, John D. Pountney and Joseph Ring, Junior, son of the original Joseph Ring. The last-named partner died, however, before the deed could be executed and the firm carried **Carter & Pountney** on as Carter & Pountney until 1816 when Henry Carter **Pountney & Allies** retired. In the same year E. Allies joined Pountney and traded as Pountney & Allies until 1835, when the partnership was dissolved. Gabriel Goldney **Pountney & Goldney** became a partner in 1836 and the style of the firm became Pountney & Goldney until 1849 when Goldney withdrew. J. D. Pountney continued **Pountney & Co.** alone until his death in 1852, when his widow carried on alone for several years. The firm traded as Pountney & Co. during both these periods.

It is interesting to note that Joseph Ring, when he first bought the factory in 1784, travelled round several Staffordshire potteries between that date and 1787 buying their various types of wares in order to increase his stock.* Among the potteries visited was that of John Yates of Shelton, from whom he bought printed wares. As has been noted, John Yates was one of the earliest to experiment in Staffordshire with underglaze transfer-printing. By 1787, Ring was advertising that he was making Queen's and other earthenwares 'which he will sell on as low terms, wholesale and retail, as any of the best manufactories in Staffordshire can render the same to Bristol'.† It is difficult to say at what time the manufacture of blue-printed began at Bristol, as the practice of buying earthenwares from the Staffordshire Potteries continued for some time. Queen's Ware formed the main output for some years, but later enamelling was almost superseded by printed decoration. Flown-blue is said to have been a speciality.

A designer and engraver, by the name of Wildblood from Burslem, is recorded‡ as being responsible for nearly all the printed patterns made by Pountney & Allies and Pountney & Goldney. His commonest design was the Willow pattern. One series was called 'The Drama'§ (pl. 93), so named on the back in a floral scroll. Each piece

* Hugh Owen, *Two Centuries of Ceramic Art in Bristol*, 1873, p. 344
† *Ibid.*, p. 347
‡ W. J. Pountney, *Old Bristol Potteries*, 1920, p. 118
§ *See also* Rogers, John & Son, p. 94 above

had a different scene of each act, taken from a variety of plays, including Shakespeare. Another design was the 'Abbey' pattern, showing ruins, with a heavy floral border. During the Pountney & Goldney partnership he engraved the 'Bristol' series, showing different views of Bristol Harbour. Other views were Avon Gorge, a reach of the Avon, the Hotwells, etc. (pl. 94).

Most printed wares bear the impressed horseshoe shaped mark, Pountney & Allies or Pountney & Goldney (fig. 90). Other printed or impressed marks may be BRISTOL POTTERY or various initials, B.P., P. & A. or simply P.A. or P. A dish in the Victoria and Albert Museum printed in blue with the Arms of the City of Bristol, and a flower and leaf border, has a printed mark 'Bristol Pottery' in an oval medallion (pl. 92) (fig. 88). Another Bristol mark is illustrated (fig. 89).

Cambrian Pottery   Swansea. George Haynes became connected with the pottery at Swansea, trading as John Coles & Co., at some time in the early 1780s. The works were greatly enlarged by Haynes and his partners, and styled the 'Cambrian Pottery', which name remained throughout its existence. In 1802 Lewis Weston Dillwyn joined the firm, which became Haynes, Dillwyn & Co. until 1810, when Haynes withdrew from the partnership. In 1811 Timothy Bevington and his son, John, employees in **Dillwyn & Co.**   the firm, became partners, when the firm traded as Dillwyn & Co. Dillwyn retired in 1817 and sublet the works to the Bevingtons. From 1817 until 1821 **Bevington & Co.**   the Bevingtons with others ran the company as T. & J. Bevington & Co. This proved an unhappy partnership which was dissolved in 1821, leaving T. & J. Bevington to struggle on alone until 1824. In this year L. W. Dillwyn again took over the factory and resumed active operations on his own. He continued until 1831, when his son, Lewis Llewelyn Dillwyn, although very young, was nominally in control. This continued until 1850 when the factory was sublet to Evans & Glasson until 1862. The firm then became D. J. Evans & Co. until 1870 when the factory was closed down.

George Haynes engaged some workmen from Staffordshire, including Thomas Rothwell (*q.v.*), decorator, engraver and printer. The Cambrian Pottery produced a fine white earthenware at this time, much of which was decorated with blue underglaze transfer-printing; most of this printing is thought to be designed by Rothwell, including some pseudo-Chinese garden scenes. Dated jugs and other pieces of this period, late eighteenth or early nineteenth century, sometimes have printed verses in addition to the pattern. Early Swansea rims are often edged with a brown or orange colour. The first Willow pattern, with no willow tree, was made in large quantities before 1810 and preceded the true Willow pattern. When the firm became Dillwyn & Co. in 1811 there was a large increase in transfer-printing. In addition to the usual rural scenes, portrait pieces and attractive ship and shell designs were produced. During the Bevington period, although the output was small, transfer-printing was the main form of decoration. A few new designs were produced including an Italianate scene of tower, trees, mountains and packhorses in the foreground, but copies of old patterns were mainly used. When Dillwyn returned to the factory in 1824 there was a great revival. He concentrated on transfer-printed decoration and many new designs were produced, both in blue and other colours. His 'Bridge and Tower' design and the 'Castle' pattern were exact copies of patterns already produced by Spode. A pattern of great local interest,* the 'Ladies of Llangollen', showing two mounted women, one talking to a man with a scythe, cows, cottage, trees and a large fort-like building on the left background (pl. 95), was made in large quantities. Another attractive design has a vine-leaf background, overlaid with scattered flowers merging into a floral border. After 1831, the younger Dillwyn produced some new rural scenes including one of cows crossing a stream. New shell designs appeared and the old ship plates were made, although the border was now left plain. Colours other than blue were increasingly used: a gradual deterioration set in and the blue wares became lighter and less pleasant in colour.

Early transfer-printed pieces are often unmarked and, as elsewhere, only a few pieces of each service were marked. The most usual early mark was 'SWANSEA' impressed. The word CAMBRIAN or CAMBRIAN POTTERY is rare and was possibly used only on painted wares. Between 1811 and 1817 the usual mark was DILLWYN & CO. or D. & CO., with or without Swansea: more rarely DILLWYN & CO., SWANSEA was impressed in horse-shoe form. Between 1817 and 1824 the impressed mark was BEVINGTON or BEVINGTON & CO. When Dillwyn resumed control again in 1824 the horseshoe shaped mark may have been used again for a short time, but the more usual mark was DILLWYN, DILLWYN, SWANSEA or simply D. A large number of printed marks were used incorporating the name of the pattern or the type of body, sometimes without any indication of the maker (figs. 91 and 92). Impressed workmen's marks representing spades, clubs and diamonds were used between c. 1800 and 1810, but the spade mark has also been noted on Leeds ware (fig. 93). Marks are often accompanied by an impressed number. Six-, eight- or ten-pointed stars appear alone, or in addition to the other marks. A very complete list of patterns used, together with illustrations both of designs and marks, is given in *The Pottery and Porcelain of Swansea and Nantgarw* by E. Morton Nance.

Glamorgan Pottery Swansea. About 1813 William Baker, William Bevan, Thomas Irwin and others, with the help of George Haynes, who had severed his connection with the Cambrian Pottery in 1810, acquired the premises adjoining the Cambrian Pottery in order to start another manufactory which they called the Glamorgan Pottery Co. The firm was generally known in Swansea as Baker, Bevans & Irwin. When Irwin died in 1818, his wife became a partner and they continued to trade under the same style. Finding competition too great, the Dillwyns of the Cambrian Pottery bought out the Glamorgan Pottery in 1838, and closed it down.

* E. Morton Nance, *The Pottery and Porcelain of Swansea and Nantgarw*, 1942, p. 150, footnote 3

The Glamorgan Pottery produced considerable quantities of blue-printed earthenwares, as well as transfers in other colours. Some patterns were original but others were close copies of the more successful designs of the Cambrian Pottery. The 'Ladies of Llangollen' pattern (pl. 95) was used by this factory and is an exact copy of both the design and border and must have been taken from the same copper plates. Pseudo-oriental designs, including a Willow pattern, and the familiar rural patterns were issued. One of the more attractive engravings is a three-masted ship in full sail with a border of naval and other emblems, the mark G.P. CO. appearing in small letters on the design; otherwise 'Glamorgan Pottery Co.' never seems to have been used as a mark. The usual mark is B.B. & I. or the name BAKER, BEVANS & IRWIN, sometimes in circular form with SWANSEA at the bottom, and the Prince of Wales feathers in the middle. 'Opaque China', or the name of the pattern, often appears on printed marks. Sometimes the firm was referred to as Baker, Bevans & Co. or later as Martin Bevan & Co. During this period the mark B.B. & CO. was sometimes used.

South Wales Pottery Llanelly. About 1839 William Chambers began to erect a pottery in Llanelly. He was able to secure some of the plant and a few of the workmen from the Glamorgan Pottery, Swansea, which had closed down in 1838. He produced both painted and printed earthenwares. The pottery continued under the control of Chambers until 1854, when it came under new management. Marks may be CHAMBERS LLANELLY or SOUTH WALES POTTERY or the initials S.W.P., with or without the name CHAMBERS.

Shropshire Potteries

Caughley Shropshire. This began as a small pot-works owned by a Mr Browne which, after his death, was taken over by Ambrose Gallimore to whom, in 1754, a lease was granted for 62 years. In 1772, Gallimore was joined by his son-in-law, Thomas Turner, who had worked at the Worcester Porcelain Factory for some years, where he had learned the technicalities of both overglaze and underglaze printing. Hitherto, earthenwares only had been made at Caughley, but it was Turner's intention to enlarge the factory and produce large quantities of porcelain decorated, in the main, with blue underglaze printing. This he soon accomplished, but it is unlikely that the manufacture of earthenware had entirely ceased during this period. When a suitable earthenware body had been evolved, mainly through the efforts of Josiah Wedgwood, the Caughley works began to produce substantial quantities of a pearl ware type of body decorated with underglaze blue transfer-printing, in addition to porcelain. Traditionally the Willow pattern is said to have been the first underglaze blue transfer-printed pattern on earthenware, designed at Caughley by Thomas Minton in 1780. Another famous pattern associated with this factory is the 'Broseley dragon'.

Turner had gathered together a school of apprentices who became skilled engravers and printers and together they produced a number of patterns following the pseudo-oriental style which had become so fashionable on porcelain. For the next twenty years there followed a number of *chinoiserie* patterns, based on the familiar theme of rocks, pagodas, islands and willow trees (pl. 2). Marked specimens of Thomas Turner's earthenware have become comparatively scarce. There are however a number of unmarked pieces showing a kinship in shape, decoration and an occasional use of gilding, with Caughley porcelain, which are probably by this factory.

The same marks were used by Thomas Turner on his earthenware as on his porcelain, C or S or occasionally the name 'Salopian' in full, printed in underglaze blue.

This factory, which had made ceramic history by being the first to use underglaze printing on earthenware, continued under Turner until 1799. In that year it was acquired by John Rose as a going concern. Rose had originally been apprenticed to Turner at Caughley, and later had established a porcelain factory at Coalport on the Severn bank, nearly opposite Turner's factory. Rose continued the Caughley works in conjunction with his own until he closed them down in about 1812: they were finally pulled down in 1821. It is probable that earthenwares continued to be made at Caughley under the direction of Rose, at any rate for a few years.

Pierce, W. & Co. of Benthall, Shropshire. A pottery called the Mug House is recorded by Chaffers as being established at Benthall in 1772 by John Thursfield, when he retired from the Jackfield Works, famous for their black glazed wares. On his death the pottery was continued by his son, John Thursfield, who with his brother-in-law traded as W. Pierce & Co. until about 1818. A man called Bathurst then succeeded to the firm, but no indication of the type of wares made is given.

Derbyshire Potteries

Bromley, William of Whittington Potteries, Chesterfield, Derbyshire. These were very old-established potteries making brown stonewares in the local tradition. About 1800 they were taken by William Bromley who carried on for several years. In addition to brown stonewares, he made cream and white coloured earthenwares, including much domestic ware decorated with blue transfer-printing.

Brunt, John of Rawdon Pottery, near Burton-on-Trent, Derbyshire. This pottery was first started by John Hall, who on his failure was succeeded by John Brunt about 1830. He continued until his death, when he was followed by his son Thomas Brunt who, after a few years, failed and gave up in 1861. The name BRUNT has been recorded on useful domestic earthenwares.

Sharpe, Thomas of Swadlincote Potteries, Swadlincote, Derbyshire. These works were erected by Thomas Sharpe in 1821 and carried on by him until he died in 1838. They were then continued by his brothers as Sharpe, Brothers & Co. Among a very large variety of earthenwares some blue-printed goods were produced.

Yorkshire Potteries

Leeds Pottery Yorkshire. This pottery was established in the 1750s, the first recorded proprietors being a family named Green. In 1775 the firm became Humble, Green & Co., and shortly afterwards Humble, Hartley, Greens & Co. In 1781 the title was Hartley, Greens & Co., and continued under this style, in spite of many changes in partnership, until the firm became bankrupt in 1820. After the bankruptcy the factory was managed by Samuel Wainwright until 1825, when he was able to buy the pottery and traded under the name of Samuel Wainwright & Co. Although Wainwright died about 1833 the name remained until 1837, when trustees continued the business as the Leeds Pottery Co. until 1841. Next, Stephen Chappell, who had been the manager, bought the factory and with his brother James Chappell traded as S. & J. Chappell until their bankruptcy in 1847. Subsequently the firm became:

R. Britton & Co., 1850–3
Warburton & Britton, 1853–61
Richard Britton, 1861–72
Richard Britton & Sons, 1872–8.

The Leeds Pottery was chiefly renowned for its cream-coloured wares. The factory had produced a pearl ware body by 1790 and Joseph and Frank Kidson, in the earliest book dealing exclusively with the Leeds Pottery,[*] gave it as their opinion

* J. and F. Kidson, *Leeds Old Pottery*, 1892

that blue-printed ware was not produced before this date. Donald Towner* states that it was first produced about 1810 and most surviving marked specimens seem to suppor this view. There are, however, a few notable exceptions (pl. 96). The earliest under-glaze transfer-printing on pearl ware was in a rich sparkling tint of blue of very good quality (pl. 97). Later a lighter, more faded tint was used. The early designs were the usual *chinoiseries* including their own versions of the Willow pattern. Rustic scenes with cows, figures and cottages and romantic ruins, mansions and castles followed (pl. 98). Somewhat later, small pieces for children with scriptural and nursery rhyme subjects were made. Bat-printing in underglaze blue also occurs. Kidson states that second-hand copper plates were purchased from the Staffordshire potters, so that the same patterns can sometimes be found on Leeds and Staffordshire examples. Unlike the cream-coloured wares, on which marks are scarce, it is exceptional for blue-printed pieces not to be marked. LEEDS POTTERY in various forms of type was the most common mark used, sometimes abbreviated to L.P. More occasionally the name or initials of one of the trading names might be used.

Rockingham Works Swinton, Yorkshire. This pottery, which more correctly should be named Swinton Pottery until 1826, was established about 1745. The firm traded as Thomas Bingley & Co. in 1778: with Thomas Bingley were associated John and William Brameld and other partners. The firm became closely connected with the Leeds Pottery. In 1787 the partnership was Greens, Hartley & Co., and in 1796 it was Greens, Bingley & Co. In 1806 this partnership was dissolved and all connection with the Leeds Pottery came to an end. John and William Brameld, who had been partners in the old firm, became the sole proprietors as Brameld & Co. In 1813 William Bra-meld died and the direction of the firm was taken over by Thomas, George and John Brameld, sons of the previous owners. In 1826 the firm was in financial difficulties which, with the help of Earl Fitzwilliam, were overcome, and the factory, being on the estate of the Marquis of Rockingham, took the name 'Rockingham Works'. Becoming financially embarrassed again, the works were closed in 1842, and all manu-facture of earthenware and porcelain ceased.

Large quantities of blue-printed earthenwares were made by the Bramelds (pl. 99), sometimes showing a rather florid tendency, which might be expected from a firm mainly interested in making porcelain in keeping with the taste of the time.

The usual mark is 'BRAMELD' impressed, usually followed by a cross or a number or both. Some printed marks were used giving the name of the pattern without any distinguishing factory mark. Jewitt illustrates a dated double-handled mug† from which he deduces that blue transfer-printing of the Willow pattern type was in use as early as 1788. Considering the almost identical partners in the Swinton and Leeds potteries at the time, this would be surprising, if the latter did not use this form of

---

* Donald Towner, *The Leeds Pottery*, 1963, p. 43
† Jewitt, *op. cit.*, vol. 1, p. 495, and description p. 496

decoration until 1810. Should this be so, however, one would expect examples of this early period to be marked 'BINGLEY' or other name instead of Brameld. An unusual impressed mark is BRAMELD within a floral wreath (pl. 100).

Don Pottery Swinton, Yorkshire. This pottery was founded about 1790 by John and William Green, sons of John Green who was one of the partners in the Leeds Pottery. About 1800 John Green Senior resigned his partnership at Leeds and joined his sons as a partner at the Don Pottery, when the factory was enlarged; he died in 1805. At first the style of the firm was Green, Don Pottery and in 1807 Greens, Clark & Co. By 1822 the style was John & William Green & Co. In 1834 the Don Pottery was sold to Samuel Barker, the proprietor of the Mexborough Old Pottery (*q.v.*). About 1850 the firm became S. Barker & Son and continued until almost the end of the century.

The wares produced at this pottery were similar to those made at Leeds, but blue-printed wares appear to have been made to a much larger extent. The patterns followed the usual trend, *chinoiseries*, rustic scenes and a few more original designs with rather pretentious borders (pl. 102). A series of named Italian antiquities, mostly of tombs, obelisks etc., had a floral and foliage border from which emerged a pair of flying cupids (pl. 101).

Early marks were impressed or printed DON POTTERY, more rarely GREEN, DON POTTERY. A later mark, sometimes impressed, but usually printed, consisted of a lion supporting a standard containing the word DON, with POTTERY appearing below (fig. 77). After 1834 Barker also used this mark with the initial B or the name BARKER. A rare mark, the word DON on a pad has been recorded on some specimens (fig. 76).

Mexborough Old Pottery Mexborough, Yorkshire. This pottery was established towards the end of the eighteenth century by Messrs Sowter & Bromley, who traded as Sowter & Co. and remained there until 1804. In that year the works were acquired by Peter Barker and later by his nephew, Samuel Barker. In 1834 Samuel Barker bought the Don Pottery and ran the two works in conjunction until 1844, when the Mexborough Old Pottery was discontinued. The factory produced the commoner types of earthenware including blue-printed. The marks of the original owners were SOWTER & CO. MEXBRO impressed or the initials S. & CO. and later BARKER, with or without the name of the pottery.

Reed & Taylor Rock Pottery, Mexborough, Yorkshire. This pottery was worked by James Reed and Benjamin Taylor as Reed & Taylor from about 1820 to 1839, when they took over the Ferrybridge Pottery near Pontefract, Yorkshire (*q.v.*). James Reed continued at the Rock Pottery as J. REED until 1849, when the works were renamed Mexbro Pottery and were carried on by his son John Reed until about 1873. The Mexbro Old Pottery (*q.v.*) had been discontinued in 1844. Marks, impressed or printed, occur with the name REED. The mark R. & T. could apply, at the various dates, to the Rock Pottery or the Ferrybridge Pottery.

Middlesbrough Pottery Middlesbrough, Yorkshire. Established in 1831, this pottery traded as the Middlesbrough Pottery Co. until 1844, when it was reconstituted and became the Middlesbrough Earthenware Co. until 1852, when the firm became Isaac Wilson & Co. These firms made large quantities of domestic wares, much of which were decorated with blue printing. In addition to their own version of the Willow pattern, they produced floral and rustic scenes and some named English landscape scenes. They made large quantities of the familiar river scene with two punts, with a bridge behind and trees and houses in the background, also made by several other potters (pl. 12). Some of these in addition to the impressed mark have a printed mark with the words 'Wild Rose' in a floral wreath, which appears to refer to the border pattern.

Marks may be M.P. & CO. or MIDDLESBRO' POTTERY. The most common form of this mark is with MIDDLESBRO' POTTERY, impressed in horse-shoe shape, arranged around an anchor (fig. 79). Sometimes the initials M.P. CO. appear with an anchor (fig. 78). Another mark recorded in many mark books is an anchor with the word LONDON* (figs. 80 and 81), but this appears to be doubtful. An impressed crown is also attributed to the Middlesbrough Pottery.† If this is correct, some very well potted pieces with well-printed views, named on the back, such as Kirkham Priory, Yorkshire (pl. 103) (fig. 99), St Albans Abbey, Hertfordshire, Furness Abbey, Lancashire, with an attractive border of flowers and scrolls may be by this pottery.

The mark M.E. & CO. would apply to the period 1844–52.

Newhill Pottery near Swinton, Yorkshire. John Twigg, who had been manager of the Swinton Pottery when it was Brameld & Co., founded Newhill Pottery in 1822. In 1839 he also acquired another small works in the vicinity, called Kilnhurst Old Pottery. Later the style became J. Twigg & Co. and both potteries operated until about 1880. White and printed earthenwares were made at both factories.

Marks were TWIGG, TWIGG NEWHILL, TWIGG K.P. or the initials J.T., all usually impressed.

Rainforth & Co. Petty's Pottery, Holbeck Moor, Leeds. Founded about the middle of the eighteenth century by Petty and Rainforth, these works stood very close to the Leeds Pottery and according to Kidson ranked next to that factory in importance. About 1792 the style became Rainforth & Co. Later alterations in title were Pettys & Co. in 1818, Petty & Hewitt in 1822, and from 1825–47 Samuel Petty & Son, after which time it became John Mills.‡ The mark Rainforth & Co. has been recorded.

* This impressed mark has been noted on blue transfer-printed pieces of good quality
† An impressed crown, in many different forms, has been noticed on so many blue-printed pieces that it was almost certainly used by other potters
‡ D. Towner, *Leeds Pottery*, 1963, p. 159

Castleford Pottery Castleford, near Leeds, Yorkshire. The Castleford Pottery was established by David Dunderdale about 1790. According to Jewitt the firm became David Dunderdale & Co. in 1803 and ceased production in 1820. Shortly afterwards the pottery was taken over by Taylor, Harrison & Co. and was subsequently worked by several different firms.

Dunderdale mainly made creamwares but is now best known for his white felspathic stonewares. Some excellent underglaze blue-printed pieces with *chinoiserie* designs were produced (pl. 104).

Marks used were D.D. & CO. CASTLEFORD or CASTLEFORD POTTERY.

Ferrybridge Pottery near Pontefract, Yorkshire. Prior to 1804 this pottery was known as Knottingley Pottery and was established in 1792 by William Tomlinson as Tomlinson & Co. In 1796 Ralph Wedgwood, a nephew of Josiah Wedgwood and already noticed as a Burslem potter, joined the firm. The partnership was Tomlinson, Foster, Wedgwood & Co., but the firm used the impressed mark WEDGWOOD & CO. In 1801 Wedgwood dissolved the partnership and the firm reverted to the style Tomlinson & Co. until 1834, when it became Tomlinson, Plowes & Co. In 1840 Reed & Taylor (*q.v.*) of the Rock Pottery, Mexborough, worked the Ferrybridge Pottery as Reed, Taylor & Kelsall. In 1843 Kelsall retired and the firm continued as Reed & Taylor until 1856. Jewitt notes that they made blue-printed. Apart from the Wedgwood & Co. mark used between 1796 and 1801 the usual marks were TOMLINSON & CO. or FERRY-BRIDGE. After 1840 Reed & Taylor used the same mark as at Mexborough, R. & T.

Belle Vue Pottery Hull, Yorkshire. James and Jeremiah Smith, potters of Hull, are said by Jewitt to have entered into partnership with Josiah Hipwood and Job Ridgway of Shelton in November 1802. The same authority also states that in 1806 Job and George Ridgway took over complete control of the works for several years as sole proprietors. As Job Ridgway died in 1813 and George Ridgway in 1823, it is not very clear what happened until 1826, when the pottery was taken over by William Bell who remained there until the pottery was closed down in 1841.

The output of these works is said to have been very large, including much blue-printed (pl. 105). If the Ridgway connection is correct, one would expect this type of decoration to have been used at an early date.

The name BELLE VUE appears on some printed marks. Two different versions of two bells printed or impressed appear as marks with or without the name of the pottery (figs. 73 and 74). At what time this mark was introduced is uncertain. Whether it was inspired by the Ridgways after the name of their own Bell Works at Shelton, or by William Bell when he took over control in 1826, is debatable, but can possibly be best decided by the type of ware on which the mark appears.

Smith, William & Co. Stafford Pottery, Stockton-on-Tees. Strictly in Durham, but lying on the border of Durham and Yorkshire on the opposite bank of the River Tees to Middlesbrough, this pottery is included with the group of potteries to which it is more nearly related.

Established in 1825 by William Smith, who traded as William Smith & Co. until 1855, when the firm became G. Skinner & Co. They made wares for domestic use mainly in creamware, but also blue-printed white wares. The mark was W.S. & CO. STAFFORD POTTERY. Cases occur where the name WEDGWOOD, WEDGEWOOD or VEDGWOOD is included in the mark (pl. 106). In 1848 an injunction was granted to Messrs Wedgwood of Etruria restraining them from using these marks.

Lancashire Potteries

Bolton, James & Fletcher   of Warrington, Lancashire. These two brothers started this pottery about 1797. They engaged Joseph Ellis of Hanley, an experienced potter who had been apprenticed to Josiah Wedgwood, as the managing partner. They employed workmen from Staffordshire and established a good trade with America. Dwindling trade with that country, and the American war of 1812, caused their failure and final bankruptcy in 1812. Jewitt describes a variety of wares which they made, including blue and white-printed wares, but very few appear to have been marked.

Herculaneum Pottery   Liverpool, Lancashire. Richard Abbey, with a partner named Graham, founded a pottery in Liverpool in 1793. In 1796 the factory was sold to Messrs Worthington, Humble & Holland, who named it the Herculaneum Pottery. In 1806 the works were enlarged and further capital acquired by an increase in the number of partners, but continued under the same management. In 1833 the company sold out to Thomas Case and John Mort who traded as Case, Mort & Co. until 1836 and then Mort & Simpson until the factory closed in 1841.

Richard Abbey learnt the art of engraving and printing with Sadler & Green of Liverpool. Afterwards he went first to a pottery in Glasgow, and later to a manufactory in France to teach the art of engraving. It is probable that all the printed wares during his three years at the Liverpool factory were overglaze transfers. When Messrs Worthington, Humble & Holland took over in 1796, they engaged several Staffordshire workmen and concentrated on producing underglaze blue transfer-printed white and cream-coloured wares. About 1800 porcelain was also made and immense quantities of all their products were shipped to North America.

Jewitt states that 'the first productions of the Herculaneum Works were confined to blue-printed ware, in which dinner, toilet, tea and coffee services, punch bowls, mugs and jugs were the principal articles made; and cream-coloured ware, which was then so fashionable'.* Mayer, in greater detail, says 'the first ware made here Nov. 11, 1796 was blue-printed and had the name "HERCULANEUM" painted in blue at the bottom of it. The first piece made was a chamber-pot.'† A punch bowl dated 1796 (pl. 108), although unmarked, is attributed by the authorities of the Liverpool Museum to Herculaneum and may, therefore, be one of the first pieces of blue-printed made at this pottery.

The factory issued many excellent patterns on a hard white body with a good glaze. Some pieces have openwork rims, others have a raised scalloped edge. Two interesting documentary pieces, also in the Liverpool Museum, printed with the same design, are a spoon tray and plate (pl. 107). The former has an impressed mark H.P. 1809; and the latter HERCULANEUM in small capitals. One attractive series was a set of sporting prints (pl. 109), duck shooting, etc., similar to some of the earlier overglaze black prints of Sadler & Green. The blue prints have various floral borders, the rose being prominent. Another service had views of the principal towns in England, including Oxford (pl. 110) and Cambridge, the name of the town being printed in blue on the bottom of the piece in a cartouche peculiar to this factory (fig. 87). The border to these pieces is the usual Liverpool floral type, but quartered with medallions of boys with a classical vase (pl. 111). A later series, usually marked with the impressed 'Liver Bird' of the Case & Mort period, or after, consists of local views in Liverpool.‡ These have the names on the back such as 'Royal Institution, Liverpool', 'Liverpool from the Mersey', 'The House of Correction, Kirkdale, Liverpool', the 'Fort and Lighthouse', 'Lord Street' and 'Castle Street, Liverpool' (pl. 112). The borders are made up of scattered bouquets of flowers. Many other services, including toy sets, have Indian and Far Eastern scenes, again with floral borders, and usually with impressed marks HERCULANEUM in large capitals or HERCULANEUM curved round a crown. Bat-printing was also practised on earthenware bodies, including a good series of contemporary celebrities such as Nelson, Wellington, etc.

Early pieces, if marked, usually have the name HERCULANEUM impressed in small or large capitals, often with a workman's or pattern number attached. This name may be printed or even painted. Other marks were HERCULANEUM in a garter with a crown in the centre (figs. 82 and 83) or Liverpool above an anchor (fig. 84). These may be impressed or printed. By a resolution of the Committee of Management dated 6 August 1822, already quoted, it was made obligatory for all pieces manufactured to be conspicuously marked HERCULANEUM POTTERY. Case & Mort & Co. are said to have

* Jewitt, *op. cit.*, vol. 2, p. 47

† Joseph Mayer, *On the Art of Pottery with a history of its progress in Liverpool*, 1873, p. 87

‡ Many of the views of Liverpool are derived from engravings in *Lancashire Illustrated*, 1832. I am indebted to Mr Alan Smith, Keeper of Ceramics and Applied Art at the City of Liverpool Museums, for this and other information

introduced the mark of the 'Liver Bird', either by itself or in a scroll, impressed or printed, in 1833 (figs. 85 and 86).

Durham Potteries

Sunderland Potteries   Durham.

An important group of potteries was established in, or around, Sunderland towards the end of the eighteenth century. These are chiefly known, and their wares collected, for their products decorated with lustre and overglaze black printing. Rhymes and mottoes were a speciality. All of them used underglaze blue printing, and most of them produced their own version of the Willow pattern, but services decorated solely with blue printing were the exception, and very few appear to have survived.

The chief potteries were:

Ford Pottery   South Hylton, Sunderland. This pottery was operated by John Dawson in 1799. Later his sons Thomas and John Dawson joined the business and by 1837 it was known as Thomas Dawson & Co. Little of any merit appears to have been produced after 1848 and the works were closed down in 1864.

Among a large variety of wares a certain amount of blue-printed was made (pl. 115), including a Willow pattern. Impressed or printed marks contain the name DAWSON, or the name of the pottery FORD or LOWFORD and sometimes both.

North Hylton Pottery   Sunderland. Established in 1762 by William Maling, the management of the works was entrusted to John Phillips. In 1780 the style of the firm was given as Phillips & Maling. In 1815 the management was taken over by the Phillips family (Robert Maling having transferred to a pottery in Newcastle) and the title became John Phillips and remained in the family until 1867 when the pottery closed down. The usual mark was J or JOHN PHILLIPS, HYLTON POTTERY or HYLTON POTWORKS.

Southwick Pottery   Sunderland. Established by Anthony Scott in 1788, in partnership with his father Henry Scott and Edward Atkinson, the firm was conducted as Atkinson & Co. until 1799. In 1800 the title became Anthony Scott & Co. until 1829, when it changed to A. Scott & Sons. When Anthony Scott retired in 1841 the firm traded as Scott Bros & Co. and, after one or two more changes of title, closed down in 1896.

The marks, usually impressed, show the name of the firm at the various dates.

Sunderland or Garrison Pottery   This pottery was leased by John Phillips of the North Hylton Pottery (*q.v.*) in 1807 and operated in his sole name until 1812. From 1813 until 1819 the style was Phillips & Co. and/or Dixon & Co. From 1820–6 this became Dixon, Austin & Co., 1827–40 Dixon, Austin, Phillips & Co. and lastly Dixon, Phillips & Co., from 1840 to 1865, when the pottery ceased. This pottery produced a very large variety of earthenwares including a certain number of blue-printed patterns.

Marks show the name of the various partnerships, often accompanied by SUN-DERLAND or SUNDERLAND POTTERY.

Wear Pottery   Sunderland. This pottery was in the possession of John Brunton from 1789 until 1803, when it was taken over by Samuel Moore in partnership with Peter Austin, trading as S. Moore & Co. In spite of many changes of ownership, this trading name was retained until the pottery closed down in 1881 (pl. 114).

The name or initials always appeared on the mark and sometimes included SUNDERLAND or the name of the pattern.

Detailed information of these Sunderland potteries and their wares is given in *The Potteries of Sunderland and District* issued by the Sunderland Public Libraries, Museum and Art Gallery, edited by J. T. Shaw (2nd revised edition issued in 1961).

Northumberland Potteries

Newcastle Potteries   Northumberland
Carr's Hill Pottery   Gateshead, Newcastle-upon-Tyne. This pottery was established about the middle of the eighteenth century by John Warburton and remained in this family until it closed down in 1817. Very little information is available of the types of ware made. Marks are recorded of the name WARBURTON with N. ON TYNE or N. C. TYNE.

Newcastle or Forth Banks Pottery   Newcastle-upon-Tyne. Jewitt records this pottery as being started by Addison & Falconer about 1800. He gives the successive owners as Redhead, Wilson & Co. and then T. Wallace & Co. The *Encyclopaedia of British Pottery and Porcelain Marks* gives the dates of Wallace & Co. as 1838–93. Chaffers records a blue-printed plate with the impressed mark WALLACE & CO.

Ouseburn Pottery Newcastle-upon-Tyne. Robert Maling (already noted at the North Hylton Pottery, Sunderland) established this pottery in 1817. He was succeeded by his son C. T. Maling in 1853. They made lustre and printed wares similar to those made at Sunderland. The mark was MALING impressed. Some similar type wares with the impressed letter 'M' have been attributed to this factory. Late blue-printed wares bear the impressed mark C. T. MALING and a printed mark with the name of the pattern and the initials C.T.M.

Sheriff Hill Pottery Newcastle-upon-Tyne. This pottery appears to have been operated from about 1820 by a firm named Ford & Patterson and later from about 1830 by Jackson & Patterson. They also used the style Patterson & Co. Chaffers records two marks, one printed in blue PATTERSON & CO., and the other impressed J. & P.

St Anthony's Pottery Newcastle-upon-Tyne. This pottery was established about 1780, but little is known of its early history. About 1804 it passed into the hands of a family named Sewell. About 1830 the trading name was Sewell & Donkin until the middle of the century when it became Sewell & Co. They made a large variety of earthenwares much of which was decorated with overglaze or underglaze printing, including blue-printed. Jewitt* records some interesting particulars of their wares and printing processes, furnished by a former manager of the works.

The earliest mark was the name of the pottery ST ANTHONY'S impressed. From about 1804, impressed or printed marks take the name of the firm: SEWELL, SEWELL & DONKIN, SEWELL & CO.

St Peter's Pottery Newcastle-upon-Tyne. Established in 1817 by Thomas Fell and Thomas Bell the firm traded as Thomas Fell & Co., and continued until 1869 when it became a limited company. They made ordinary domestic ware, including blue-printed. Marks include FELL, F. & CO., T.F. & CO. and T. FELL & CO. and sometimes the name FELL or the initial F with an anchor. Chaffers records a mark of the arms of the town of Newcastle printed in blue with the name FELL on the label below the shield.

Stepney Bank Pottery Newcastle-upon-Tyne. Jewitt records a pottery of this name established between 1780 and 1790 for the production of common earthenware. He lists the partnerships as:

1801, Head & Dalton
1816, Dryden, Coxon & Basket
1822, Davies, Coxon & Wilson
1833, Dalton & Burn, who were succeeded by G. R. Turnbull.

* Jewitt, *op. cit.*, vol. 2, p. 6

Tyne Pottery Newcastle-upon-Tyne. The *Encyclopaedia of British Pottery and Porcelain Marks* records a short-lived pottery making earthenwares, worked by Taylor & Co. (alternatively Tyler & Co.) about 1820–5 and which by 1827 was listed as Taylor & Son. Rare printed marks have been recorded of the name of the firm with TYNE POTTERY, NEWCASTLE. The name of the firm appears in one case as part of the printed decoration.

Tyne Main Pottery Newcastle-upon-Tyne. Jewitt records this pottery as built in 1833 by R. Davies & Co., making white, printed and lustre ware. It was closed in 1851.

Scottish Potteries

Scotland has always had a surprising number of potteries. These have been dealt with in detail by J. Arnold Fleming in *Scottish Pottery*, published in 1923. Many of the potteries followed the prevailing trend and made use of the new and cheaper form of decoration, underglaze blue printing, often with the help of potters recruited from Staffordshire.

Some of the most important, specimens of whose wares may sometimes be found, are as follows:

Bo'ness Potteries (Borrowstounness). John Roebuck acquired this pottery in 1786 and, importing finer clays from England, made cream-coloured and white wares. When he died a few years later the pottery was taken over first by McCowen and in 1799 by Alexander Cummings, who was succeeded by his nephew J. C. Cummings. Later still the factory was purchased by Shaw & Sons and in 1836 was sold again to Jameson & Co. Fleming states that workmen, including printers, were engaged from Staffordshire at this period and excellent blue and white ware was made. The firm remained under this management until 1854, when Jameson died.

Clyde Pottery Greenock. These works were built in 1816 by two brothers, Andrew and James Muir, who traded as Andrew Muir & Co. They employed James Stevenson (*see also* Greenock Pottery) as manager and made a variety of earthenwares, including blue-printed. In 1840 Thomas Shirley joined the firm from Staffordshire as a partner and shortly afterwards acquired the business and traded as Thomas Shirley & Co. He disposed of the works to the Clyde Pottery Co. in 1857. Most early wares appear to have been unmarked. Printed and impressed marks are CLYDE, GREENOCK, C.P. CO. in a garter, often with the name of the pattern. T.S. & CO. was used from 1840–57.

Greenock Pottery Greenock. These works were established at Ladyburn, Greenock, about 1820 by James Stevenson, previously noted as the manager of the Clyde Pottery, Greenock. At some time after 1830, Stevenson sold the business to the Shirleys of the Clyde Pottery, who in 1849 disposed of it to Clough & Geddes, who changed the name to Ladyburn Pottery. The impressed or printed mark was GREENOCK POTTERY. Fleming assigns the impressed mark STEVENSON over a ship inside a narrow oval garter to James Stevenson c. 1820–30. This mark has been noted under Andrew Stevenson of Cobridge to whom it is normally attributed (fig. 60).

Gordon's Pottery Prestonpans. Dating from the early eighteenth century, this pottery operated until it closed in 1832. Blue- and white-printed ware is said to have been one of the features of this pottery. The initials ' G.G.' sometimes appear on printed marks, being those of one of the Gordon family, who owned the pottery during the whole of its existence. Occasionally GORDON impressed was used, but marked pieces are rare.

Scott Brothers Portobello. The Scott brothers opened this pottery about 1786, but closed it in 1796. Shortly afterwards it was reopened by Cookson & Jardine, who announced that the works were being reconstructed along Staffordshire lines. In 1808 the factory was sold to Thomas Yoole (or Yuille). In 1810 it was taken over by Yoole's son-in-law, Thomas Rathbone, who traded as Thomas Rathbone & Co. The pottery remained under this management until just before the middle of the century. Figures were the main output of the factory, but blue printing was employed to some extent. Marks were T. RATHBONE, T.R. & CO.

Thomson, John of Annfield Pottery, Glasgow. This pottery was built about 1816. John Thomson is said to have been closely connected with Staffordshire and engaged most of his staff and potters from Burslem. White earthenwares were produced in large quantities, much of it being transfer-printed. About 1865 the firm became John Thomson & Sons and the works closed in 1884. Early marks were J.T. and J.T. ANNFIELD

Verreville Pottery Glasgow. As the name implies, this pottery was originally a glasshouse but began making pottery towards the end of the eighteenth century. In 1806 the factory was sold to John Geddes, who had previously been the manager of the works. In 1824 the firm traded as John Geddes & Son and in 1827 as Geddes, Kidston & Co. This continued until 1834, when Geddes dissolved partnership and the style became Kidston, Cochran & Co. In 1847 Cochran took over as Robert Cochran & Co., which remained the style of the firm until 1918. The names or initials of the various partnerships may appear on impressed or printed marks, sometimes with the name of the pottery. A large export trade was carried on with America and printed earthen-

wares have been recorded in America with the printed mark

JOHN GEDDES
Verrville
Pottery

Watson's Pottery Prestonpans. These works were erected by the Watson family about the middle of the eighteenth century. Getting into financial difficulties, they were aided by John Fowler about 1820, when the firm became Fowler, Thomson & Co. The pottery ceased production in 1840. Underglaze blue printing was in use at least by 1810. They made a Willow pattern and other designs, including one called 'Bird and Fly'. Early marks were WATSON impressed or in printed marks WATSON & CO. After about 1820 FOWLER, THOMSON & CO. appears either printed or impressed.

Supplementary List of Potters

INITIAL and name marks still turn up which are impossible to apply to any of the recorded potters. Many short-lived potteries and partnerships have disappeared without trace: many others of whom merely the name and place and perhaps a single date at which they were in operation have survived. Most of the following list of potters fall within this last category. Where the mark does not appear to apply to any of the better-known potters, this list may provide a possible solution provided that the approximate date of the piece and that of the potter can be reconciled. The names and dates have been gathered from various directories or any other available source, including the early historians of English ceramics. The source from which they are taken is quoted in each case, but it must be remembered that the early records are fallible and the spelling is sometimes phonetic rather than accurate.

Adams, James, Burslem; Engraver, 1802—Chaffers

Allason, John, Seaham Pottery, Sunderland; 1838–41. This name and pottery have been recorded as marks on blue-printed wares—*The Potteries of Sunderland and District*, p. 25

Arkinstall & George, Burslem; 1802—Chaffers

Ashwell & Cooper, Lane End, Longton; c. 1841—Ward

Bacchus, William, Fenton; 1786—Chaffers

Bagley, William, Burslem; 1786—Chaffers

Bagnall, Sampson, Hanley; 1786—Chaffers. He died in 1803

Bagnall & Hull, Lane Delph; 1802—Chaffers

Bagshaw, Sam, Basford, Newcastle-under-Lyme—1818 directory*

Bailey & Ball, Longton; c. 1843–50—*Encyclopaedia of British Pottery and Porcelain Marks*,† p. 710

Bailey, Goodwin & Robey, Lane End; c. 1841—Ward

Baker, Samuel (two factories), Lane Delph; 1802—Chaffers

Ball, Richard, Burslem; 1802—Chaffers

Barnes, George, Lane End; 1802—Chaffers. Probably the potter referred to by Jewitt (vol. 2, p. 399) as G. Barnes who established the St Gregory's Pottery, Longton in 1794 and later became

Barnes & Wood

Barton & Swift, Burslem; c. 1811—*Encyclopaedia*, p. 712

Batkin & Deakin, Waterloo, Flint Street, Lane End—1818 directory

Bedson & Rhodes appear in a list of Burslem and Tunstall and Cobridge earthenware

---

* Published in Josiah C. Wedgwood, *Staffordshire Pottery and its History*
† Abbreviated in all following cases to *Encyclopaedia*

potters at a meeting in Burslem on 30 April 1795—Frank Falkner, *The Wood Family of Burslem*, 1912, p. 64

Bell, J. & M. P., Glasgow Pottery, Glasgow; c. 1842 onwards—Fleming, p. 133

Bell, Sarah, Stoke; 1786—Chaffers

Berks, J. & W., Lane End; 1802—Chaffers

Bettany & Tomlinson, Lane End; 1843-4—*Encyclopaedia*, p. 712

Bill, John. An earthenware potter of Lane End who died in 1836—Chaffers

Bill & Lawrence, Lane End; c. 1832—*Encyclopaedia*, p. 711

Bill & Proctor, Tunstall; c. 1841—Ward

Billings & Hammersley, Hanley; 1802—Chaffers

Birch, Joseph, Hanley; c. 1847-51—*Encyclopaedia*, p. 723

Booth & Marsh, Shelton; 1802—Chaffers

Bowers, G. F., Brownhills Works, Tunstall; 1842-68—*Encyclopaedia*, p. 93 and Chaffers. Makers of porcelain and earthenwares. These initials appear in various forms, sometimes in a Staffordshire knot—Jewitt, vol. 2, p. 429

Bowers & Lloyd, Burslem; c. 1846—*Encyclopaedia*, p. 711

Boyle, Samuel & James, Church Street, Stoke; c. 1842-3—*Encyclopaedia*, p. 120

Bradshaw, Jos., Booden Brook, Cobridge—1818 directory

Bradshaw, Joseph, Booden Brook, Hanley—1818 directory

Breeze, William, Shelton; c. 1812-20—*Encyclopaedia*, p. 99

Breeze & Co., Tunstall—mentioned by Shaw, p. 17, and probably refers to Jessie Breeze who had died in 1826. *See* main section, John Breeze

Breeze & Wilson, Hanley; c. 1809-17—*Encyclopaedia*, p. 75

Brian, Lane End, Longton; c. 1841—Ward. *See* Riddle & Lightfoot

Bridgwood & Burgess, Longton; c. 1846-7—*Encyclopaedia*, p. 710

Brindley, James, Stoke; 1786—Chaffers

Brindley, John & Co., Hanley; c. 1824-30—*Encyclopaedia*, p. 723

Brindley, Taylor, Fenton; 1786—Chaffers

Brooks, Philip & Co., Sitch, Burslem—1818 directory

Brough, Benjamin Singleton, Lane End; c. 1810—Chaffers. *See* Johnson & Brough in main list

Brough, Thomas, Green Dock, Lane End—1818 directory

Brown, Henry & Co., Lane End; c. 1828-30—*Encyclopaedia*, p. 313

Brownfield, W. & G., Keelings Lane, Shelton, Hanley—1818 directory

B. T. P. Co. These initials are sometimes found on blue-printed wares of quite good quality and refer to The Bovey Tracey Pottery Co. of Bovey Tracey, Devon, who operated for about half a century beginning in 1842

Capper, John & Thomas, Golden Hill, Tunstall; 1802—Chaffers

Cartledge, James, Golden Hill, Tunstall—1818 directory

Cartledge, Richard, Golden Hill, Tunstall—1818 directory

Cartlidge, S. & J., Burslem; 1786—Chaffers

Cartledge & Beech, Knowle, Burslem—1818 directory and mentioned by Ward c. 1841 as discontinued

Cartlich, Samuel & Thomas, Tunstall; 1802—Chaffers; also mentioned as being present at a meeting of Burslem and Tunstall earthenware potters on 30 April 1795 —Frank Falkner, *The Wood Family of Burslem*, 1912, p. 64

Chatterley, C. & E., Hanley; 1786—Chaffers. Fl. 1780. Charles died in 1786, Ephraim in 1811. Succeeded by J. & W. Handley

Chelenor & Adams, Fenton; 1802—Chaffers. Probably a mistake for Challinor & Adams. Challinor became a well-known potter's name later in the century

Chesworth & Robinson, Lane End; 1825–40—*Encyclopaedia*, p. 143, formerly

Chesworth & Wood—Jewitt is evidently referring to this firm at St Gregory's Pottery, Longton in vol. 2, p. 399

Close, Valentine, Hanley; 1802—Chaffers. In conjunction with James Keeling (*q.v.*) he patented improvements in ovens, kilns and processes of firing in 1796—Jewitt, vol. 2, pp. 328 and 525. c. 1783–1810

Clowes, William, Longport, Burslem; c. 1783–96—*Encyclopaedia*, p. 153 and presumably the same potter who was connected with the New Hall porcelain factory for a time as a sleeping partner—Jewitt, vol. 2, pp. 302–4

Clowes & Williamson, Fenton; 1786—Chaffers

Clulow, Robert & Co., Lower Lane, Fenton; 1802—Chaffers

Colclough, Lane End, Longton; c. 1841—Ward

Cole, Caleb & Co., Newfield, Tunstall; 1802—Chaffers; also mentioned as being present at a meeting of Burslem and Tunstall earthenware potters on 30 April 1795 —Frank Falkner, *The Wood Family of Burslem*, 1912, p. 64

Colli*s*on, John, Golden Hill, Tunstall; 1802—Chaffers, probably a misprint for

Colli*n*son, Jas., Golden Hill, Tunstall—1818 directory

Copestake, William, Junr., Lane End, Longton; c. 1834–60—*Encyclopaedia*, p. 735; Ward, evidently referring to the same firm, gives two factories:

Copestick, W., Junr., Lane End; c. 1841

Copestick, W., Senr., Lane End; c. 1841

Coxon, Harding & Co., Cobridge; c. 1841—Ward, probably in error for Harding & Cockson of Cobridge (*q.v.*), not to be confused with Cockson & Harding of Shelton —*see* Hackwood, Thomas

Davenport, Charles, Burslem; 1802—Chaffers

Dawson, Samuel, Lane End, 1802—Chaffers

Dawson, William, Burslem; 1802—Chaffers

Dimmock, James & Co., Hanley; c. 1840–50—*Encyclopaedia*, p. 724

Downing, William, Old Hall Lane, Hanley; Engraver, 1802—Chaffers

Drury, T. & Son, Daisy Bank, Lane End—1818 directory

Elkin & Newbon, Longton; c. 1844–5—*Encyclopaedia*, p. 234

Emery, James, Mexborough, Yorkshire; 1837–61—*Encyclopaedia*, p. 237

Everard, Colclough & Townsend, Lane End, c. 1837–45—*Encyclopaedia*, p. 241;
  listed as Everard, Townsend & Colclough by Ward c. 1841
Everard & Glover, Lane End; c. 1846
Everard, Glover & Colclough, Lane End; c. 1847
Floyd, Benjamin, Anchor Lane, Lane End; c. 1843—*Encyclopaedia*, p. 252
Ford, Hugh, Green Dock, Lane End—1818 directory
Forrester & Meredith, Lane End; 1786—Chaffers
Forster, John, Hanley; c. 1820—*Encyclopaedia*, pp. 257–8
Gibson, John, Tunstall; c. 1841–6—*Encyclopaedia*, p. 724
Gilbert, John, Burslem; 1802—Chaffers
Goddard & Salt, Lane End, Longton; c. 1841—Ward
Godwin, B. C., Burslem; c. 1851, and possibly of Cobridge as early as 1836—
  Encyclopaedia, p. 277
Godwin, James, Cobridge; c. 1846–50—*Encyclopaedia*, p. 724
Godwin, Rathbone & Co., Market Place, Burslem; c. 1822—*Encyclopaedia*, p. 278
Godwin, Rowley & Co., Market Place, Burslem; 1828–31—*Encyclopaedia*, p. 278
Graham, John, Junr., Burslem; 1786—Chaffers
Greatbatch, James, Shelton; 1802—Chaffers
Green, John, Burslem; 1786—Chaffers
Guest, Thomas, Burslem; 1802—Chaffers
Hackwood, Josiah, Hanley; 1842–3—*Encyclopaedia*, p. 299
Hall, Samuel, Shelton, Hanley; c. 1841–56 and probably as early as 1834—*Encyclo-
  paedia*, pp. 303 and 731
Hall & Holland, Tunstall; 1838–43—Ward and *Encyclopaedia*, p. 721; *see* Hall, Ralph
Hallam & Co., Longton; c. 1845–8—*Encyclopaedia*, p. 720
Hamilton, Samuel & Co., Lane End; c. 1840 —*Encyclopaedia*, p. 731
Hamilton & Moore, Lane End, c. 1841—Ward, and probably the same firm which
  Jewitt refers to at St Mary's Works, Mount Pleasant, Longton as Moore & Hamilton,
  1830–52—vol. 2, p. 384
Hammersley, John, Shelton; 1802—Chaffers
Hampson & Broadhurst, Longton; c. 1847–53—*Encyclopaedia*, p. 721
Hancock & Wright, Tunstall; c. 1841—Ward
Handley, J. & W., Hanley; c. 1810—Jewitt
Hanson, Thomas & Co., Hanley; c. 1841—Ward
Harris & Hulme, Longton; 1840–1—*Encyclopaedia*, p. 721
Harvey, Bailey & Co., Lane End; 1833–5—*Encyclopaedia*, p. 313
Hassels, John, Shelton; 1786—Chaffers
Hawley, Lane End, Longton; c. 1841—Ward
Hawley, John & Co., Foley Pottery, Fenton; 1842—Ward, and was still occupied
  by W. Hawley & Co. when Jewitt wrote in 1878—vol. 2, p. 410
Hawley, Joseph, Waterloo Road, Burslem; c. 1841—Ward

Heath, Samuel & Co., Lane End; c. 1831—*Encyclopaedia*, p. 731

Hewit, John, Lane End; 1802—Chaffers

Hewitt, John & Son, Green Dock, Lane End—1818 directory

Hewitt & Buckley, Booden Brook, Shelton; 1802—Chaffers

Hewitt & Comer, Lane End; 1802—Chaffers

Hobson, Ephraim, Cobridge—1818 directory

Holdcroft, Peter & Co., Burslem; 1846–52—*Encyclopaedia*, p. 328

Holdcroft & Box, Cobridge—1818 directory

Holden, John, Knowl Works, Burslem; c. 1846—*Encyclopaedia*, p. 329

Hollings & Co., Brook Street, Shelton—1818 directory

Hopkin, Peter, Market Place, Burslem; c. 1841—Ward

Hopkins & Co., Burslem; c. 1841–3—*Encyclopaedia*, p. 720

Horn, John, Brimleyford, Tunstall; 1802—Chaffers

Hulme & Harris, Longton; 1840–1—*Encyclopaedia*, p. 721; possible alternative for Harris & Hulme (*see* above)

Indeo Pottery, Bovey Tracy, Devon; c. 1772–1841—*Encyclopaedia*. 'Indeo' impressed mark appears very rarely on earthenwares. An underglaze blue-printed creamware plate is illustrated by Geoffrey A. Godden, *An Illustrated Encyclopaedia of British Pottery and Porcelain*, pl. 322

Ingleby, Thomas & Co., Tunstall; c. 1834–5—*Encyclopaedia*, p. 346

Jarvis, Ric., Nile Street, Burslem—1818 directory

Kennedy, William Sadler, Washington Works, Burslem; 1843–54—*Encyclopaedia*, p. 369, Jewitt, vol. 2, pp. 257–8

Knight, T. & J. Clayhill, Tunstall—1818 directory

Leak, Jonathan, Waterloo Works, Burslem; c. 1800—G. W. Rhead, *British Pottery Marks*, p. 157; said to have established the first pottery in Australia—Jewitt, vol. 2, p. 282

Ledge, Charles, Sleek Lane, Hanley; Engraver, 1802—Chaffers

Lees, Joseph, Hanley; 1802—Chaffers

Leigh, George & Ralph, Cobridge; c. 1841—Ward

Leigh, Isaac, Burslem; 1802—Chaffers

Lindop, John, Green Lane, Tunstall; 1802—Chaffers

Lomas, George, Hanley; c. 1841—Ward; *see* Barlow & Hammersley in main list

Lowe, W. & J., Church Street, Lane End—1818 directory

Lowndes & Hill, Stoke;—listed by Ward c. 1841 as 'at present void'

Lucock, John, Lane Delph; 1802—Chaffers; probably a partner of Thomas Wolfe & Miles Mason (*q.v.*) c. 1795

Lucock, John, Stoke; listed as an engraver, 1802—Chaffers

Machin, Jonathan, Chell, Tunstall; 1802—Chaffers

Malkin, Burnham, Burslem; 1786—Chaffers

Mansfield & Hackney, Cobridge; c. 1828—Shaw

Mansfield, Pawley & Co., Market Place, Shelton—1818 directory

Marsh & Halls appear in a list of earthenware potters present at Burslem on 30 April 1795 at which potters from both Tunstall and Burslem were present. Frank Falkner, *The Wood Family of Burslem*, 1912, p. 64

Martin, George, Commercial Street, Burslem; Engraver, 1802—Chaffers

Massey, Nehemiah, Bournes Bank, Burslem; c. 1841—Ward

Massey, Ric., Castle Street, Burslem—1818 directory

Massey, S. & T., Nile Street, Burslem—1818 directory

Mathers & Ball, Lane End—1818 directory

Mayer, John, Foley; 1833–41—*Encyclopaedia*, p. 423; mark given as $\begin{smallmatrix} J & M \\ & F \end{smallmatrix}$

Mayer, Samuel & Co., Waterloo Road, Burslem; c. 1841—Ward

Mayer & Mawdesley, Tunstall; c. 1841—Ward. The *Encyclopaedia* gives the dates of this firm as 1837–8.

Meakin & Proctor, Lane End; c. 1845—*Encyclopaedia*, p. 727

Mear, John, Tunstall; c. 1828—Shaw. The firm referred to is almost certainly John Meir (*q.v.*)

Mills & Fradley, Shelton; c. 1827–35—*Encyclopaedia*, p. 726

Mollart, John, Shelton; Engraver, 1802—Chaffers

Morris, Thomas, Marsh Street, Shelton—1818 directory

Mort, Barker & Chester, Burslem; 1802—Chaffers

Moss, T. & H., Red Street, Tunstall—1818 directory

Moss & Henshall, Red Street, Tunstall; 1802—Chaffers

Nixon & Whalley, Tunstall—1818 directory

Nutt, William, Flint Street, Lane End—1818 directory

Oliver & Bourne, Cobridge—1818 directory

Palin & Co. A mark recorded on blue-printed earthenwares in the *Encyclopaedia*, p. 727, but no other information of this firm is available

Peover, Fred, High Street, Hanley—1818 directory of earthenware potters. The *Encyclopaedia* gives the dates as 1818–22 as a manufacturer of porcelain only

Perry, Samuel, Hanley; 1786—Chaffers

Phillips, Thomas & Son, Burslem; c. 1845–6—*Encyclopaedia*, p. 493

Pope, Thomas, Shelton; 1802—Chaffers

Poulson, Thomas, Hanley; c. 1825–6—*Encyclopaedia*, p. 734

Poulson, William, Chancery Lane, Lane End—1818 directory

Poulson & Dale, Stoke—1818 directory

Powis, H. & Co., Sandiford, Tunstall—1818 directory

Proctor, John, Longton; 1843–6—*Encyclopaedia*, p. 516

Ratcliffe, Mrs, Stoke Lane, Stoke; 1802—Chaffers

Ratcliffe & Blood appear without an address in a list of Staffordshire potters in the *Belle Vue Papers* in 1823—Chaffers

Rathbone & Brummitt, Tunstall; c. 1841—Ward

Ray & Tideswell, Lane End, Longton; c. 1830–46—*Encyclopaedia*, p. 525

Ray & Wynne, Lane End, Longton; c. 1841—Ward; Jewitt, vol. 2, p. 404, states that Ray & Wynne succeeded Ray & Tideswell at the Daisy Bank Works, Longton

Read & Goodfellow, Burslem; 1802—Chaffers; *see* Bathwell & Goodfellow in main section. The firm *Rh*ead & Goodfellow appears on an interesting list of potters supplying goods to Abbott & Mist (*q.v.*), London dealers at some time between 1801–8—Bevis Hillier, *The Turners of Lane End*, p. 64

Reade, Samuel & George, Stoke; Earthenware potters, c. 1841—Ward

Riddle & Bryan, Longton; c. 1835–40—*Encyclopaedia*, p. 532

Riddle, James & Co., Lane End, Longton; c. 1841—Ward

Riddle & Lightfoot, Lane End; c. 1842–51—*Encyclopaedia*, p. 532

The above three entries refer to the same firm, George Bryan having withdrawn from the firm in 1840

Ridgway, Smith & Ridgway, Shelton; c. 1793–1800—*Encyclopaedia*, p. 730

Riles & Bathwell, Tunstall; 1802—Chaffers (*see* Bathwell & Goodfellow in main section)

Robinson, John, George Street, Lane End—1818 directory

Robinson, John, Burslem; 1786—Chaffers

Robinson, J. & C., Hill Top Works, Burslem—1818 directory

Robinson & Sons, Burslem; 1802—Chaffers

The above three Robinsons of Burslem are, according to Jewitt, a continuation of the same firm founded by John Robinson, who had left Sadler & Green of Liverpool to begin his own pottery about 1786. George Robinson & Sons appear on a list of Burslem and Tunstall potters in 1795

Robinson & Dale, Lane End, Longton; c. 1841—Ward

Robinson & Smith, Cobridge; 1786—Chaffers. This firm also appears on a list of earthenware potters in 1795

Rowley, Thomas, Tunstall; c. 1841—Ward

Ryles, Moses, Lane End; Engraver, 1802—Chaffers

Shelley, Michael, Lane End; 1786—Chaffers

Shelley, Thomas, Lane End; 1786—Chaffers

Shelley, Thomas, Lane End; 1802—Chaffers

Shelley, Booth & Co., Lane End—1818 directory

Shelly, Thomas, Lane Delph; 1802—Chaffers

Sheridan, J. H., Union Market Place, Lane End—1818 directory

Shirley, Lindop & Co., Longport; 1802—Chaffers

Shufflebottom, William, Little Fenton; Engraver, 1802—Chaffers

Simpkin & Waller, Lane End—1818 directory

Simpson, Nicholas, Shelton; c. 1821–4—*Encyclopaedia*, p. 732

Simpson & Wright, Shelton; 1802—Chaffers

Smith, John & Joseph, Burslem; 1786—Chaffers. Joseph Smith was present at a meeting of Burslem and Tunstall potters in 1795

Smith, Theophilus, Smithfield Works, Tunstall; c. 1791–7. Theophilus Smith was present at a meeting of Burslem and Tunstall potters in 1795. He committed suicide whilst in prison on a charge of attempted murder in 1800. The works were taken over in 1797 by John Breeze (*q.v.*) and renamed Greenfield

Smith & Billington, Cobridge; 1802—Chaffers

Smith & Jarvis, Stoke; 1802—Chaffers

Smith & Steel, Tunstall; 1802—Chaffers

Sparks, Thomas, Stoke; Engraver, 1802—Chaffers

Spode, Samuel, The Foley Works, Foley, Fenton; 1802—Chaffers. He was succeeded by Charles Bourne (*q.v.*)

Stanley, John, Hanley; 1802—Chaffers

Stanley, William, Knowle Works, Burslem—1818 directory

Stanley, William & John, Burslem; 1802—Chaffers

Stevenson, Charles & Son, Burslem; 1786—Chaffers

Stevenson, Alcock & Williams, Cobridge; c. 1825—*Encyclopaedia*, p. 597; probably another partnership of the better-known firm of R. Stevenson & Williams (*q.v.*)

Swift & Elkin, Longton; c. 1841—Ward. The *Encyclopaedia*, p. 606, gives the dates as 1840–3, succeeded by J. Swift

Taylor, John & Co., Burslem; 1802—Chaffers

Taylor, William & Co., Cobridge; c. 1834–45—*Encyclopaedia*, p. 737

Taylor & Pope, Shelton; 1786—Chaffers

Tellwright & Co., Burslem; 1802—Chaffers

Tompkinson, Sam, Church Street, Burslem—1818 directory

Tunstall, Thomas, Golden Hill, Tunstall; 1802—Chaffers

Unett, John, High Street, Lane End—1818 directory

Vernon, James & Co., High Street, Burslem; c. 1841—Ward

Vernon, Samuel, Shelton; Engraver, 1802—Chaffers

Walklete, Mark, Lane End; 1786 and 1802—Chaffers

Walkl*a*te, H. & R., High Street, Lane End—1818 directory

Walsh, William, Furlong, Burslem—1818 directory

Ward, William, Lane End; 1802—Chaffers

Ward & Co., Stoke—1818 directory

Ward & Forrister, Stoke; c. 1829—Shaw

Warren, James, Longton; c. 1841–53—*Encyclopaedia*, p. 723

Warren & Adams, Lane End, Longton; c. 1841—Ward

Wedgwood, Thomas (1762–1826), Overhouse and Bighouse Works, Burslem, 1786, and Overhouse Works, 1802—Chaffers

Wedgwood & Johnson, High Street, Burslem—1818 directory

Weston, George, High Street, Lane End—appears on lists in 1802 and 1818

Weston, T., on list of potters in 1823 with no address but probably of Lane End—Chaffers

White, Thomas, Hanley; c. 1840–1—*Encyclopaedia*, p. 734

White, William, Hanley (late Poulson); c. 1841—Ward; *see* Thomas Poulson of Hanley in supplementary list

Whitehead, Dorothy, Shelton; 1802—Chaffers

Whitehouse, Edward, Little Fenton; Engraver, 1802—Chaffers

Williams, Thomas, Stoke; c.1827—*Encyclopaedia*, p. 734

Wood, Ephraim, Hole House, Burslem—1818 directory

Wood, William & Co., Burslem; 1802—Chaffers

Wood & Bowers, Waterloo Road, Burslem; c. 1841—Ward. The *Encyclopaedia*, p. 683, gives the date as 1839

Woodnorth & Co., an impressed mark reported on rare printed wares, one with a subject engraved by James Brindley, dated 1819. The *Encyclopaedia*, p. 736, states that Brindley was working at Burslem at this period, but that there is no record of this firm

Worthington, Thomas, Hanley; c. 1842—*Encyclopaedia*, p. 734

Wright, Thomas, Hanley; 1786—Chaffers

Wright, Thomas, Hanley; c. 1822–5—*Encyclopaedia*, p. 734

Wynne, Thomas, Longton; c. 1850–1—*Encyclopaedia*, p. 734

Index

Marks

Most marks consist of the names or initials of the potter or firm, either printed or impressed. These can be by themselves, or forming part of a more complicated pattern. It is obviously impossible to illustrate more than a small fraction of the marks used by the hundreds of potters on blue-printed earthenwares. The following have been chosen either as being typical of the better-known makers of this class of ware, or as scroll-, wreath- or cartouche-type marks used for containing the pattern name or type of body, which are peculiar to certain potteries and which often appear without the potter's name and can therefore be useful in determining attribution. A few of the cartouche and scroll marks illustrated still await attribution.

1 & 2   Impressed marks of William Adams of Stoke-on-Trent.

3–7   Various scroll, cartouche and wreath marks of William Adams of Stoke used to contain the title of the view or pattern. A variety of other scroll or wreath marks were also used.

Marks

8 & 9   Impressed marks of J. & R. Clews of Cobridge.

10   Printed cartouche design used by J. & R. Clews of Cobridge for titles of Dr Syntax series.

11   A mark occasionally found on blue-printed wares of J. & R. Clews presumably c. 1820 or 1830.

12   A printed seal mark of J. & R. Clews of Cobridge.

13   Printed design of J. & R. Clews for the 'Select Scenery' series.

14   Printed mark attributed to Baggerley & Ball of Longton. This basic form of mark was used by several potters to contain their initials.

15   Staffordshire knot mark of William Brownfield of Cobridge 1850+.

16   The printed mark of T. & J. Carey of Lane End for their 'Cathedral' series, usually accompanied by the impressed name 'CAREYS' above an anchor.

17   Printed Royal Arms mark on blue-printed wares of Jonathan Lowe Chetham of Longton, 1841–62.

18   Printed mark of Cork & Edge of Burslem.

19   Printed cartouche mark of Deakin & Bailey of Lane End.

20   A variety of printed marks in this form with the initials E. B. & Co. were used by Edge, Barker & Co. of Fenton and Lane End.

8

9

10

11

12

13

14

15

16

17

18

19

20

21 Marks used by two of the several partnerships of Elkins, Knight & Co. of Fenton (*see also* Fig. 103).

22 Printed scenic mark of Thomas Godwin of Burslem with space reserved for title of pattern.

23 Cartouche mark of Thomas & Benjamin Godwin of Burslem.

24 Cartouche mark of John Hall of Burslem with space reserved for title of pattern.

25 & 26 Cartouche marks of Ralph Hall of Tunstall.

27 Wreath mark of Henshall & Co. of Longport, Burslem.

28 & 29 Two Prince of Wales' three-feather crest marks of Charles Heathcote & Co. of Lane End, sometimes used without the name of the firm.

30 Royal Arms mark of Hicks & Meigh of Shelton. A different version, not so detailed and with the words 'Stone China' slightly curved, was later used by Hicks, Meigh & Johnson. The pattern number varies.

31 Crown mark of Hicks, Meigh & Johnson of Shelton.

32–4 Various marks of Hilditch & Son of Lane End.

ELKIN
KNIGHT & Co
E K B
Canton Views
OPAQUE
CHINA

21

T.G.

22

T&BG
SEMI CHINA

23

I. HALL

24

Italian
Buildings
R. HALL

25

R. HALL'S
SELECT VIEWS
Stone China

26

YORK
MINSTER

27

C. HEATHCOTE & Co

28

29

STONE CHINA
Nº 13

30

31

H S

32

H & S
Nº 4

33

H & S

34

35	Mark of Lockett & Hulme of Lane End.
36 & 37	Seal marks of Miles Mason of Lane Delph, used with or without the name.
38	Impressed mark of Thomas Mayer of Stoke.
39	Wreath mark of Edward & George Phillips of Longport.
40 & 41	Marks of George Phillips of Longport. Fig. 40 may also have been used by Edward & George Phillips.
42 & 43	Printed and impressed marks of William Ratcliffe of Hanley.
44–6	Various marks of John & Richard Riley of Burslem.
47	Seal marks with an 'R' in the centre are attributed to Job Ridgway of Shelton, Hanley.
48–50	Cartouche and wreath marks of John & William Ridgway of Shelton, Hanley.
51	A mark used by William Ridgway, Son & Co. of Hanley.
52	One of the cartouche marks of William Ridgway of Shelton, Hanley.
53	The mark of Rogers of Longport is sometimes accompanied by the sign for Iron or Mars. This sign may appear without the name.
54 & 55	Arrow marks with or without the letter 's' attributed by some authorities to Shorthose of Hanley.

35

36

37

38

39

40

41

42

43

44

45

46

47

48

49

50

51

52

53

54

55

56 Seal-type mark of Spode of Stoke. Sometimes only the bottom half of the seal appears.

57 Printed title of one of Spode's 'Indian Sporting' series, often unaccompanied by the name of the firm. Copeland & Garrett later used these same title marks, but in addition these appear always to have the impressed mark 'COPELAND & GARRETT' in circular form below a crown with the name of the body 'New Fayence' in the centre.

58 Impressed or printed mark sometimes seen on Spode wares.

59 Impressed mark of Andrew Stevenson of Cobridge.

60 Impressed mark attributed to Andrew Stevenson of Cobridge. J. Arnold Fleming *Scottish Pottery*, gives this mark to James Stevenson of the Greenock Pottery.

61 Printed mark attributed to Andrew Stevenson of Cobridge.

62 Impressed mark of Ralph Stevenson of Cobridge.

63 & 64 Printed scroll marks of Ralph Stevenson & Williams of Cobridge during their short partnership c. 1825. Enoch Wood & Sons of Burslem used a mark very similar indeed to fig. 63.

65 Impressed mark of Joseph Stubbs & Kent of Longport.

66 Impressed mark of Joseph Stubbs of Longport.

67 Impressed or printed mark of John Turner of Lane End after he had been appointed potter to the Prince of Wales in 1784.

68 Impressed mark of Enoch Wood & Sons of Burslem.

69 One of the cartouche marks used by Enoch Wood & Sons of Burslem.

70 One of the wreath marks used by Enoch Wood & Sons of Burslem.

71 Cartouche mark of Tams & Co.

72 Impressed mark of Enoch Wood & Sons of Burslem.

56

58

CHASE AFTER A WOLF.

57

62

60

61

63

64

59

67

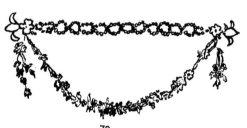

65 66

68

69

70

71

72

153

73 & 74   Impressed or printed marks of the Belle Vue Pottery, Hull.

75   Impressed or printed mark of J. & M. P. Bell, Glasgow (*see* supplementary list). The bell was sometimes used without name or initials.

76 & 77   Impressed or printed marks of the Don Pottery, Swinton, Yorkshire.

78 & 79   Marks of the Middlesbrough Pottery Co., Middlesbrough-on-Tees, Yorkshire.

80 & 81   Marks attributed by many authorities to the Middlesbrough Pottery Co.

82–4   Impressed or printed marks of the Herculaneum Pottery, Liverpool.

85 & 86   Impressed or printed marks introduced at the Herculaneum Pottery, Liverpool by Case, Mort & Co. in 1833.

87   Cartouche used for view names by the Herculaneum Pottery, Liverpool.

88 & 89   Marks of the Bristol Pottery.

90   Impressed mark during the Pountney & Goldney partnership at the Bristol Pottery. A similar type of mark was used by Pountney & Allies from 1816–35

91 & 92   Two of several cartouche and scroll marks used by the Cambrian Pottery, Swansea to contain the type of body, often without any further mark.

93   Impressed workmen's tally marks sometimes found on Swansea earthenwares. The spade-like mark has also been reported on Leeds ware.

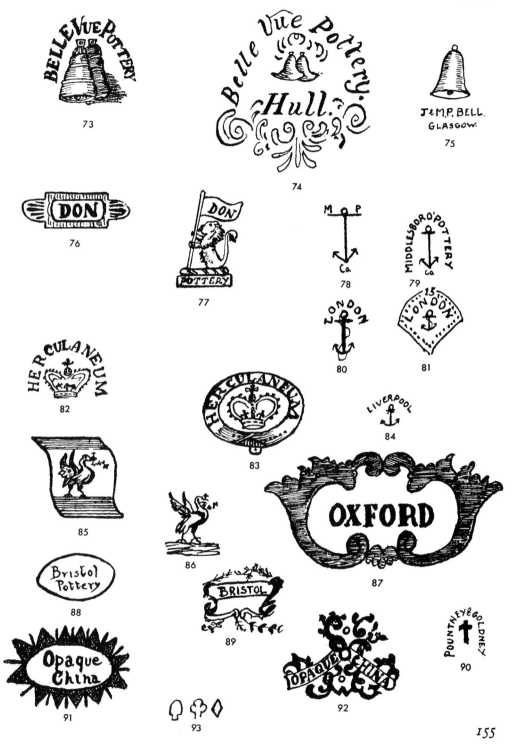

73

74

75

76

77

78

79

80

81

82

83

84

85

86

87

88

89

90

91

92

93

94 A printed design used by Phillips of Longport.

95–8 Printed view name scroll and cartouche marks on blue-printed earthenwares so far unattributed (*see* pls. 83, 86, 87 and 117).

99 Printed mark sometimes appearing with an impressed crown usually attributed to the Middlesbrough Pottery Co.

100 Printed scroll mark on dish (*see* pl. 90) so far unattributed.

101 Printed cartouche mark used by John Rogers & Son of Longport.

102 Printed cartouche mark used by Joseph Stubbs of Longport, Burslem.

94

95

96

97

98

99

100

101

102

103 Printed pre-1837 Royal Arms mark of Elkins & Co.

104 Printed Staffordshire knot mark with initials 'c. & r.', probably that of Chetham & Robinson of Lane End, but possibly of Chesworth & Robinson of Lane End (*see* supplementary list).

105 A printed mark commonly seen but apparently not yet identified (*see* Hillcock & Walton).

106 & 107 Two of the many printed marks used by John Ridgway of Shelton, Hanley, with or without the initials J. R.

108 Printed mark awaiting attribution (*see* pl. 91).

103

104

105

106

107

108

Illustrations

Although every conceivable article was made and decorated with underglaze blue printing, the greater part of the pieces chosen for illustration are plates and dishes. These show more clearly the border patterns, which can often be helpful in determining attribution.

1 Porcelainous dish, transfer-
printed in underglaze blue at
Derby. Probably engraved and
printed by Richard Holdship,
c. 1765.

2 Plate, early Willow-type
pattern used at Caughley by
Thomas Turner 1780–90. Mark:
transfer-printed C-shaped open
crescent.

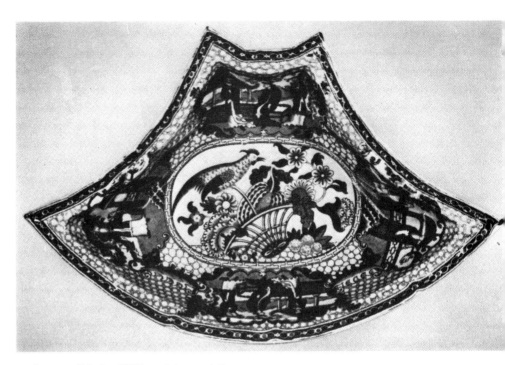

3 Supper-dish, by William Adams of Greengates, Tunstall. Mark: ADAMS impressed.

4 Fruit basket stand, with pierced border, by Benjamin Adams of Greengates, Tunstall, said to have been designed by William Brooke(s) after a picture by Claude Lorraine. Mark: B. ADAMS impressed.

Plate, 'Villa in Regent's Park,
London', by William Adams of
Stoke-on-Trent. Impressed mark:
fig. 1. Printed mark: fig. 3.

6   Plate, 'St Catherine's Hill near
    Guildford', tree and foliage border
    with scroll edge, by William
    Adams of Stoke-on-Trent.
    Impressed mark: fig. 2.

7 Plate, 'Alnwick Castle, Northumberland', tree and foliage border with scroll edge, by William Adams of Stoke-on-Trent. Impressed mark: fig. 1.

8 Plate, 'Bamborough Castle, Northumberland', border of bell- and chrysanthemum-type flowers, by William Adams of Stoke-on-Trent. This border was also used by J. & R. Clews. Impressed mark: fig. 2. Printed mark: floral wreath containing name of view.

9 Plate, 'Cupid' series with one of
the various centre designs all with
the same floral border, by William
Adams of Stoke-on-Trent.
Impressed mark: fig. 2.

10 Dish, one of the animal series
by William Adams of Stoke-on-
Trent and Greenfield. Impressed
mark: ADAMS.

11 Dish, 'Spanish Marriages Madrid', by William Adams of Stoke-on-Trent and Greenfield. Impressed mark: ADAMS.
Printed mark: W. ADAMS & SONS within a garter with title of design in the centre.

12   Jug, height 28 in., by Bourne, Baker & Bourne of Fenton, made for Bailey, Neale & Co. of St Paul's Church Yard, London, c. 1830. This pattern was later used by a great number of potters.

13 Plate, printed with the well-known Spode 'Blue Italian' pattern, by Zachariah Boyle of Hanley and Stoke. Impressed mark: BOYLE.

14 Dish, 'St Paul's Cathedral', by Thomas & John Carey of Lane End. Impressed mark: CAREYS above an anchor. Printed mark: fig. 16.

Plate, with view in quatrefoil-shaped panel, probably by Chetham & Robinson of Longton, but possibly by Chesworth & Robinson of Lane End (*see* supplementary list). Printed mark: fig. 104.

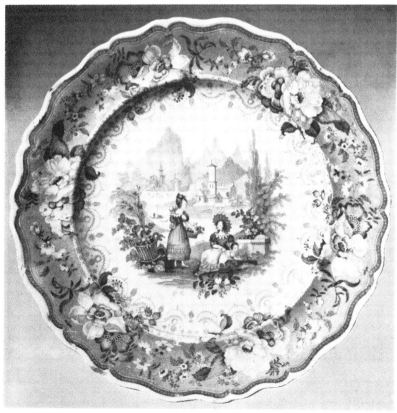

16 Plate, 'The Offering', probably by Chetham & Robinson of Longton, but possibly by Chesworth & Robinson of Lane End (*see* supplementary list). Printed mark: 'The Offering C & R' with 'TERNI' in a label across a landscape above.

17 Plate, design of romantic
ruins, by J. & R. Clews of
Cobridge. Impressed mark:
fig. 9.

18 Dish, one of a series called
'Select Scenery' of Windsor, by
J. & R. Clews of Cobridge.
Printed mark: fig. 13; otherwise
unmarked.

19　Sauce-boat stand, one of Dr Syntax series 'Death of Punch', by J. & R. Clews of Cobridge. Printed mark: fig. 10; otherwise unmarked.

20　Plate, one of Dr Syntax series 'Painting a Portrait', by J. & R. Clews of Cobridge. Impressed mark: CLEWS WARRANTED STAFFORDSHIRE (fig. 8). Printed mark: Doctor Syntax Painting a Portrait in cartouche similar to fig. 10.

21 Small dish, unusually printed
    with two scenes in reverse and
    scroll edge border, by J. & R.
    Clews of Cobridge. Impressed
    mark: fig. 8.

22 Plate, *chinoiserie* design, by
    John Davenport of Longport.
    Impressed mark: Davenport in
    lower-case letters.

23 Plate, rustic design, by John Davenport of Longport. Impressed mark: Davenport in lower-case letters above an anchor.

24 Plate, printed with design by William Brooke(s) of Port Vale, Wolstanton (*q.v.*), in dark blue, by Davenport of Longport. Impressed mark: DAVENPORT above an anchor.

25 Sauce-boat dish, 'Irish Scenery', by Elkins & Co. of Fenton. Printed mark: fig. 103.

26 Plate, 'SURSEYA GHAUT KHANIPORE', by Thomas and Benjamin Godwin of Burslem. Printed mark: T.B.G. and pattern name in a floral wreath. The same pattern name has been noted over an impressed crown.

27 Part of a toy dinner service, by William Hackwood of Eastwood, Hanley. Impressed mark: HACKWOOD.

28 Dish with perforated rim, one of 'Italian Buildings' series, by Ralph Hall of Tunstall. Printed mark: fig. 25.

29 Dish strainer, exotic bird and
floral pattern, by Harveys of
Longton.
Impressed mark: HARVEY.

30 Soup plate, cattle and river
pattern with fan border, by
Charles Heathcote & Co. of
Lane End. Impressed mark:
HEATHCOTE
 & CO. 3.

31 Plate, Buffalo pattern, probably engraved by Thomas Minton (*q.v.*), by J. Heath of Hanley c. 1790. Several potters used the same design, including Spode and Leeds. Impressed mark: I.H.

32 Sauce-boat with Buffalo pattern and an unusual mark, presumably by the same potter as pl. 31. Mark: I.H. in raised moulded letters.

33 Plate, 'York Minster', by
Henshall & Co. of Longport.
Printed mark: fig. 27.

34 Plate, one of a series of 'British
Views' by Henshall & Co. of
Longport. Impressed mark:
Henshall & Co. Printed mark:
fig. 27, with BRITISH VIEWS within
the wreath.

35 Plate with scalloped rim
attributed to Henshall & Co.

36 Tureen, with floral pattern and slight gilding, by Hicks, Meigh & Johnson of Shelton.
Printed mark: fig. 30, with pattern number 51.

37 Plate, Willow pattern, by Miles Mason of Lane Delph. Impressed mark: M. MASON.

38 Tureen, with typical Masons Ironstone China pattern. Printed mark: MASON'S above a crown and PATENT IRONSTONE CHINA in a scroll below.

39 Plate, landscape in octagonal frame with border of architectural fragments, one inscribed 'Bentley Wear & Bourne Scpt'. Impressed mark: MASON'S CAMBRIAN ARGIL.

40 Dish, by Thomas Lakin of
    Stoke. Impressed mark: Lakin in
    lower-case letters.

41 Plate, with Eastern scene,
    possibly by Richard Newbold of
    Lane End. Printed mark:
    cursive 'N'.

42 Dish, one of a series of Arms of American States, by Thomas Mayer of Stoke. Note wheel device in border pattern. Impressed mark: fig. 38. Printed mark: large eagle with E PLURIBUS UNUM on scroll beneath.

43 Plate, part of child's service with gardening print, by John Meir of Tunstall. Impressed mark: MEIR.

44 Plate, with moulded patterns on rim, made at the Operative Union Pottery, Burslem. Impressed mark: OPERATIVE UNION POTTERY.

45 Pickle dish, Willow pattern, by Phillips of Longport. Impressed mark: fig. 40.

46a   Plate, 'Pastoral Scene', in flown blue by Phillips of Longport. Printed mark: fig. 94.
46b   Plate, with the same pattern in medium blue. This and 46a have been identified from similar
       pieces bearing the name Phillips, Longport. Unmarked.

47   Dish, 'Eton College', by George Phillips of Longport. Printed mark: fig. 41. The same view and
      a similar basic mark were later used by another potter with initials not yet identified.

48 Cup and saucer, Willow
pattern in very faint blue, by
William Ratcliffe of New Hall
Works, Shelton. Printed mark:
fig. 42.

49 Plate, with early *chinoiserie*
pattern, probably made by John
and George Rogers of Longport,
for James Donovan of Dublin
(*q.v.*). Impressed mark:
DONOVAN. Some pieces of the
same pattern bear an impressed
mark ROGERS in addition to
DONOVAN.

50 Dish, 'Theatre Printing House, etc. Oxford', by J. & W. Ridgway of Shelton, Hanley. Printed mark: fig. 49 with name of view in the centre.

51 Plate, 'Radcliffe Library, Oxford', by J. & W. Ridgway of Shelton, Hanley. Printed mark: fig. 49 with name of view in the centre.

52 Dish strainer, with scene after Claude Lorraine, by J. & R. Riley of Burslem. Printed mark: fig. 44.

53 Plate, with floral design, by
J. & R. Riley of Burslem.
Impressed mark: RILEY. Printed
mark: fig. 46.

54 Dish, Chinese scene, by
J. & R. Riley of Burslem.
Unmarked.

55 Dish, 'Boston State House', by John Rogers & Son of Longport, Burslem. Rogers made three different views of Boston State House, each with a different border. Impressed mark: ROGERS.

56 Plate, one of a naval series with shell border, by John Rogers & Son of Longport. Unmarked.

57 Plate, 'Tivoli', by John Rogers & Son of Longport. Impressed mark: ROGERS. Printed mark: fig. 101.

58 Plate, Eastern scene, by John
Rogers & Son of Longport.
Impressed mark: ROGERS.

59 Plate, one of 'The Drama'
series, by J. Rogers & Son of
Longport, printed on the front
'Love in a Village Act 1.
Scene 4'. Impressed mark:
ROGERS. 8. Printed mark: THE
DRAMA within a wreath.

60 Dish strainer, Castle pattern in very light blue, by Josiah Spode II of Stoke-on-Trent. Impressed mark: SPODE. 13. Printed mark: SPODE. D.

61 Plate, Lucano pattern after an engraving of the Bridge of Lucano published in 1798, by Josiah Spode II of Stoke-on-Trent. This same pattern was used by several potteries, including those at Bristol and Swansea. Unmarked.

62 Plate, 'Chase after a Wolf',
one of the 'Indian Sporting'
series, by Josiah Spode II of
Stoke-on-Trent. Impressed
mark: SPODE. 5. Printed mark:
SPODE. B, and fig. 57.

63 Jug, by Copeland & Garrett of Stoke-on-
Trent. Printed mark: COPELAND & GARRETT in
circular form below a crown with NEW
FAYENCE in the centre.

64 Dish, pastoral scene, by
Andrew Stevenson of Cobridge.
Impressed mark: fig. 60.

65 Plate, 'Waterworks,
Philadelphia', by R. Stevenson
& Williams of Cobridge. Printed
mark: fig. 63 with name of view
on the scroll.

66 Plate, 'Fair Mount, near Philadelphia', by Joseph Stubbs of Longport, Burslem. Impressed mark: STUBBS. Printed mark: fig. 102.

67 Plate, by Toft & May of Hanley. Impressed mark: TOFT & MAY.

68 Plate, with early-type engraving of
The Archery Lesson, c. 1800.
Unmarked, but almost certainly by
William & John Turner of Lane End.

69 Sauce-boat dish with perforated rim,
Willow-type pattern, by Turner of
Lane End. Impressed mark: TURNER.

5

70　Dish, 'Post Office Dublin', showing the now-demolished Nelson column. Impressed circular mark: TAMS ANDERSON & TAMS . . . . POTTERY. Printed mark: fig. 71.

71 Plate, with view of Drury Lane Theatre, by Tams & Co. Unmarked.

72 Plate, rustic scene, by Wedgwood of Etruria. Unmarked.

73   Dish, with harbour shipping
scene, by Wedgwood of
Etruria c. 1830. Impressed
mark: WEDGWOOD.

74   Plate, one of a series of
botanical flowers, by Wedgwood
of Etruria. Impressed mark:
WEDGWOOD ETRURIA.

5　Plate, early Willow pattern, by Thomas Wolfe of Stoke. Impressed mark: Wolfe in lower-case letters.

76　Plate, with view of the State House, Boston, by Wood & Caldwell of Burslem c. 1818. Impressed mark: WOOD & CALDWELL.

77 Dish, 'Bank of England', by Enoch Wood & Sons of Burslem. Printed mark: fig. 69.

78 Plate, 'Guy's Cliff,
Warwickshire', by Enoch Wood
& Sons of Burslem. Impressed
mark: fig. 72. Printed mark: a
floral scroll with name of view
very similar to fig. 63.

79 Cup and saucer, bird pattern with border on saucer and inside the cup of interlacing circles, by
Enoch Wood & Sons of Burslem. Impressed mark: on saucer—fig. 68.

80 Plate, with COMMODORE MACDONNOUGHS VICTORY printed on the front, by Enoch Wood & Sons of Burslem. Impressed mark: fig. 68.

81 Plate, 'Lafayette mourning at the Tomb of Washington', by Enoch Wood & Sons of Burslem. Unmarked.

82   Teapot, with impressed w at base of handle, labelled by the Victoria & Albert
     Museum authorities 'c. 1800, perhaps by Warburton of Hot Lane, Cobridge'. If
     the w is intended as a mark it could equally well apply to Wolfe of Stoke or E.
     Wood of Burslem, both of whom were potting at this time.

83   Dish, one of a series called 'Metropolitan Scenery', showing 'North End,
     Hampstead'. Impressed mark: G.C. Printed mark: fig. 97.

84 Miniature plate, diameter
2¾ in., probably made at
Swansea as an advertisement for
John Mortlock's retailing and
decorating establishments in
London (*see* pl. 85).

85 Miniature plate, reverse of
above, with name of John
Mortlock's representative used
as a trade card.

86 Dish, showing view of Richmond, with very good quality printing, so far unattributed. Printed mark: fig. 95.

87 Dish, with another view of Richmond with a Ridgway type of medallion border, so far unattributed. Printed mark: fig. 96.

88   Dish strainer, of the Durham
     Ox copied from an engraving by
     J. Whessell after a painting by
     T. Boultbee, published in 1802,
     so far unattributed. Unmarked.

89   Plate, another version of the
     Durham Ox (*see* pl. 88).
     Unmarked and so far
     unattributed.

90   Dish, 'Domestic Cattle', so far
unattributed. Printed mark:
fig. 100.

91   Plate, 'Hop Pickers', so far
unattributed. Printed mark:
fig. 108.

92 Dish, printed with the arms of
the city of Bristol, by the Bristol
Pottery. Printed mark: fig. 88.

93 Plate, one of the series called
'The Drama' inscribed on the
front MIDAS ACT I SCENE 3 (*see*
pl. 59), by Pountney & Goldney
of Bristol. Impressed mark:
fig. 90. Printed mark: THE
DRAMA in a wreath, and '3'.

94 Dish, 'Bristol Hot Wells', made at Bristol Pottery in the Pountney & Allies period, and said to have been engraved by Wildblood. Printed mark: BRISTOL HOT WELLS and '18' impressed.

95 Plate, with Ladies of Llangollen pattern, made at Swansea. This pattern was produced at both the Cambrian and Glamorgan Potteries during the 1820–30 period. Unmarked.

96 Mug, creamware, with parrot and fruit design after a print by R. Hancock of Worcester, by Leeds Pottery 1790–1800. Impressed mark: LEEDS∗POTTERY.

97   Soup plate, with Buffalo
     pattern in rich sparkling blue,
     typical of Leeds Pottery to which
     it is attributed by the Victoria &
     Albert Museum authorities.
     Unmarked.

98   Plate, of later date, made at
     Leeds Pottery. Impressed mark:
     LEEDS * POTTERY.

99 Plate, octagonal with rustic scene, made at the Rockingham Works, Swinton, Yorkshire. Impressed mark: BRAMELD + I.

100 Mug, with fishing scene, made at the Rockingham Works, Swinton, Yorkshire. Impressed mark: BRAMELD within a floral wreath.

101 Plate, one of an Italian series inscribed on the front 'Tomb of Theren, Aggrigentun' (*sic*), made at the Don Pottery, Swinton, Yorkshire. Impressed mark: DON POTTERY. Printed mark: fig. 77.

102 Plate, with unusual heraldic border, made at the Don Pottery, Swinton, Yorkshire. Printed mark: fig. 77.

103 Plate, 'Kirkham Priory,
Yorkshire'. Impressed mark: a
crown (this is attributed by
many authorities to the
Middlesbrough Pottery, but was
certainly used by other potters).
Printed mark: fig. 99.

104 Plate, a different version of
the Buffalo pattern to the one
usually seen, by David Dunderdale of the Castleford Pottery,
near Leeds, Yorkshire. The
border pattern is very similar to
one used by Davenport
(cf. pl. 22). Impressed mark:
D. D. & CO CASTLEFORD POTTERY.

105 Plate, Willow pattern, by the Belle Vue Pottery, Hull, Yorkshire. Impressed mark: BELLE VUE POTTERY, HULL in circular form. Printed mark: fig. 74 superimposed on impressed mark.

106 Plate, with lion and cherubs pattern, by William Smith & Co. of Stockton-on-Tees. Impressed mark: WEDGEWOOD.

107 Plate and spoon tray, printed with the same pattern, by the Herculaneum Pottery, Liverpool. Impressed marks: spoon tray HP[7] 1809; plate HERCULANEUM.

A Wonder!
An honest Lawyer!!!
M:ʳ Miller's good Health.
One Bowl more and then.
.1796.

108 Punch bowl, dated 1796,
attributed to the Herculaneum
Pottery, Liverpool. Unmarked.
(One Aaron Miller is recorded
in the Liverpool Directories as
being an Attorney at Law at
39 Edmund Street in 1794. In
1796 there is no entry for Mr
Miller who had presumably
died.)

109 Plate, one of a sporting series,
by the Herculaneum Pottery,
Liverpool. Impressed mark:
HERCULANEUM.

110 Dish, 'Oxford' with
distinctive border pattern, by
the Herculaneum Pottery,
Liverpool (cf. pl. 50). Printed
mark: fig. 87.

111 Plate, 'Caernarvon Castle',
by the Herculaneum Pottery,
Liverpool. Impressed mark:
HERCULANEUM. Printed mark:
cartouche similar to fig. 87 with
name of view.

112 Dish, with view of Castle
Street, Liverpool, by the
Herculaneum Pottery, Liverpool.
Impressed mark: Liver bird
(fig. 86). Printed mark: 'Castle
Street & St George's Crescent,
Liverpool', in an octagonal
frame.

113 Plate, commemorating the
death of George III in 1820.
Unmarked.

114 Tureen stand, 'Excelsior' pattern, made by Samuel Moore & Co.,
Wear Pottery, Southwick, Sunderland. Printed mark: S. MOORE & CO.
SUNDERLAND and a figure against a mountain landscape holding a banner
bearing the word 'Excelsior'.

115 Plate, 'Romantic' pattern, made at Dawson's Low Ford Pottery,
South Hylton, near Sunderland. Printed mark: DAWSON within a
wreath.

116 Plate, Eastern scene in octagonal frame reserved on a ground of vermiculated pattern and an attractive border. Unmarked and awaiting attribution.

117 Plate, with view of the city of London churches with St Paul's Cathedral predominating and the River Thames in the foreground, awaiting attribution. Printed mark: fig. 98.

118 Plate, with coursing scene. Unmarked and awaiting attribution.

119 Plate, with floral border with the crocus predominating. Unmarked and awaiting attribution.